Singapore MATH

LEVEL **1**

Appropriate for Students in GRADES **1-2**

70 Must-Know WORD PROBLEMS

Thinking Kids®
An imprint of Carson-Dellosa Publishing LLC
Greensboro, North Carolina

Visit carsondellosa.com for correlations to Common Core, state, national, and Canadian provincial standards.

Thinking Kids®
An imprint of Carson-Dellosa Publishing LLC
PO Box 35665
Greensboro, NC 27425 USA

ISBN 978-0-7682-4011-5
18-153207784

INTRODUCTION TO SINGAPORE MATH

Welcome to Singapore Math! The math curriculum in Singapore has been recognized worldwide for its excellence in producing students highly skilled in mathematics. Students in Singapore have ranked at the top in the world in mathematics on the *Trends in International Mathematics and Science Study* (TIMSS) in 1993, 1995, 2003, and 2008. Because of this, Singapore Math has gained in interest and popularity in the United States.

Singapore Math curriculum aims to help students develop the necessary math concepts and process skills for everyday life and to provide students with the ability to formulate, apply, and solve problems. Mathematics in the Singapore Primary (Elementary) Curriculum cover fewer topics but in greater depth. Key math concepts are introduced and built-on to reinforce various mathematical ideas and thinking. Students in Singapore are typically one grade level ahead of students in the United States.

The following pages provide examples of the various math problem types and skill sets taught in Singapore.

At an elementary level, some simple mathematical skills can help students understand mathematical principles. These skills are the counting-on, counting-back, and crossing-out methods. Note that these methods are most useful when the numbers are small.

1. The Counting-On Method

Used for addition of two numbers. Count on in 1s with the help of a picture or number line.

$$7 + 4 = \mathbf{11}$$

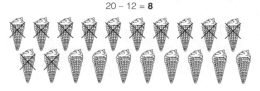

2. The Counting-Back Method

Used for subtraction of two numbers. Count back in 1s with the help of a picture or number line.

$$16 - 3 = \mathbf{13}$$

3. The Crossing-Out Method

Used for subtraction of two numbers. Cross out the number of items to be taken away. Count the remaining ones to find the answer.

$$20 - 12 = \mathbf{8}$$

A **number bond** shows the relationship in a simple addition or subtraction problem. The number bond is based on the concept "part-part-whole." This concept is useful in teaching simple addition and subtraction to young children.

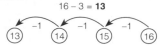

To find a whole, students must add the two parts.
To find a part, students must subtract the other part from the whole.

The different types of number bonds are illustrated below.

1. Number Bond (single digits)

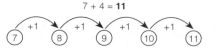

$$3 \text{ (part)} + 6 \text{ (part)} = \mathbf{9} \text{ (whole)}$$
$$9 \text{ (whole)} - 3 \text{ (part)} = \mathbf{6} \text{ (part)}$$
$$9 \text{ (whole)} - 6 \text{ (part)} = \mathbf{3} \text{ (part)}$$

2. Addition Number Bond (single digits)

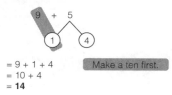

Make a ten first.

$$= 9 + 1 + 4$$
$$= 10 + 4$$
$$= \mathbf{14}$$

3. Addition Number Bond (double and single digits)

Regroup 15 into 5 and 10.

$$= 2 + 5 + 10$$
$$= 7 + 10$$
$$= \mathbf{17}$$

4. Subtraction Number Bond (double and single digits)

$$10 - 7 = 3$$
$$3 + 2 = \mathbf{5}$$

5. Subtraction Number Bond (double digits)

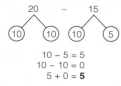

$$10 - 5 = 5$$
$$10 - 10 = 0$$
$$5 + 0 = \mathbf{5}$$

Students should understand that multiplication is repeated addition and that division is the grouping of all items into equal sets.

1. Repeated Addition (Multiplication)

Mackenzie eats 2 rolls a day. How many rolls does she eat in 5 days?

$$2 + 2 + 2 + 2 + 2 = 10$$
$$5 \times 2 = 10$$

She eats **10** rolls in 5 days.

2. The Grouping Method (Division)

Mrs. Lee makes 14 sandwiches. She gives all the sandwiches equally to 7 friends. How many sandwiches does each friend receive?

$$14 \div 7 = 2$$

Each friend receives **2** sandwiches.

One of the basic but essential math skills students should acquire is to perform the 4 operations of whole numbers and fractions. Each of these methods is illustrated below.

1. The Adding-Without-Regrouping Method

```
  H  T  O
  3  2  1        O: Ones
+ 5  6  8        T: Tens
─────────
  8  8  9        H: Hundreds
```

Since no regrouping is required, add the digits in each place value accordingly.

2. The Adding-by-Regrouping Method

```
  H  T  O
  ¹4  9  2       O: Ones
+ 1  5  3        T: Tens
─────────
  6  4  5        H: Hundreds
```

In this example, regroup 14 tens into 1 hundred 4 tens.

3. The Adding-by-Regrouping-Twice Method

$$
\begin{array}{cccc}
 & H & T & O \\
 & {}^1 2 & {}^1 8 & 6 \\
+ & 3 & 6 & 5 \\
\hline
 & 6 & 5 & 1 \\
\end{array}
$$

O: Ones
T: Tens
H: Hundreds

Regroup twice in this example.
First, regroup 11 ones into 1 ten 1 one.
Second, regroup 15 tens into 1 hundred 5 tens.

4. The Subtracting-Without-Regrouping Method

$$
\begin{array}{cccc}
 & H & T & O \\
 & 7 & 3 & 9 \\
- & 3 & 2 & 5 \\
\hline
 & 4 & 1 & 4 \\
\end{array}
$$

O: Ones
T: Tens
H: Hundreds

Since no regrouping is required, subtract the digits in each place value accordingly.

5. The Subtracting-by-Regrouping Method

$$
\begin{array}{cccc}
 & H & T & O \\
 & 5 & {}^7\!8 & {}^{11}\!1 \\
- & 2 & 4 & 7 \\
\hline
 & 3 & 3 & 4 \\
\end{array}
$$

O: Ones
T: Tens
H: Hundreds

In this example, students cannot subtract 7 ones from 1 one. So, regroup the tens and ones. Regroup 8 tens 1 one into 7 tens 11 ones.

6. The Subtracting-by-Regrouping-Twice Method

$$
\begin{array}{cccc}
 & H & T & O \\
 & {}^7\!8 & {}^9\!0 & {}^{10}\!0 \\
- & 5 & 9 & 3 \\
\hline
 & 2 & 0 & 7 \\
\end{array}
$$

O: Ones
T: Tens
H: Hundreds

In this example, students cannot subtract 3 ones from 0 ones and 9 tens from 0 tens. So, regroup the hundreds, tens, and ones. Regroup 8 hundreds into 7 hundreds 9 tens 10 ones.

7. The Multiplying-Without-Regrouping Method

$$
\begin{array}{ccc}
 & T & O \\
 & 2 & 4 \\
\times & & 2 \\
\hline
 & 4 & 8 \\
\end{array}
$$

O: Ones
T: Tens

Since no regrouping is required, multiply the digit in each place value by the multiplier accordingly.

8. The Multiplying-With-Regrouping Method

$$
\begin{array}{cccc}
 & H & T & O \\
 & {}^1 3 & {}^2 4 & 9 \\
\times & & & 3 \\
\hline
1, & 0 & 4 & 7 \\
\end{array}
$$

O: Ones
T: Tens
H: Hundreds

In this example, regroup 27 ones into 2 tens 7 ones, and 14 tens into 1 hundred 4 tens.

9. The Dividing-Without-Regrouping Method

Since no regrouping is required, divide the digit in each place value by the divisor accordingly.

10. The Dividing-With-Regrouping Method

In this example, regroup 3 hundreds into 30 tens and add 3 tens to make 33 tens. Regroup 3 tens into 30 ones.

11. The Addition-of-Fractions Method

$$
\frac{1 \times 2}{6 \times 2} + \frac{1 \times 3}{4 \times 3} = \frac{2}{12} + \frac{3}{12} = \frac{5}{12}
$$

Always remember to make the denominators common before adding the fractions.

12. The Subtraction-of-Fractions Method

$$
\frac{1 \times 5}{2 \times 5} - \frac{1 \times 2}{5 \times 2} = \frac{5}{10} - \frac{2}{10} = \frac{3}{10}
$$

Always remembers to make the denominators common before subtracting the fractions.

13. The Multiplication-of-Fractions Method

$$
\frac{{}^1 \!\cancel{3}}{5} \times \frac{1}{\cancel{9}_3} = \frac{1}{15}
$$

When the numerator and the denominator have a common multiple, reduce them to their lowest fractions.

14. The Division-of-Fractions Method

$$
\frac{7}{9} \div \frac{1}{6} = \frac{7}{\cancel{9}_3} \times \frac{\cancel{6}^2}{1} = \frac{14}{3} = 4\frac{2}{3}
$$

When dividing fractions, first change the division sign (÷) to the multiplication sign (×). Then, switch the numerator and denominator of the fraction on the right hand side. Multiply the fractions in the usual way.

Model drawing is an effective strategy used to solve math word problems. It is a visual representation of the information in word problems using bar units. By drawing the models, students will know of the variables given in the problem, the variables to find, and even the methods used to solve the problem.

Drawing models is also a versatile strategy. It can be applied to simple word problems involving addition, subtraction, multiplication, and division. It can also be applied to word problems related to fractions, decimals, percentage, and ratio.

The use of models also trains students to think in an algebraic manner, which uses symbols for representation.

The different types of bar models used to solve word problems are illustrated below.

1. The model that involves addition

Melissa has 50 blue beads and 20 red beads. How many beads does she have altogether?

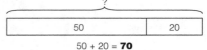

50 + 20 = **70**

2. The model that involves subtraction

Ben and Andy have 90 toy cars. Andy has 60 toy cars. How many toy cars does Ben have?

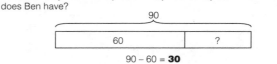

90 – 60 = **30**

3. The model that involves comparison

Mr. Simons has 150 magazines and 110 books in his study. How many more magazines than books does he have?

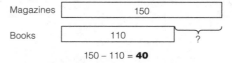

150 – 110 = **40**

4. The model that involves two items with a difference

A pair of shoes costs $109. A leather bag costs $241 more than the pair of shoes. How much is the leather bag?

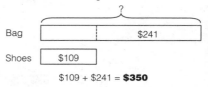

$109 + $241 = **$350**

5. The model that involves multiples

Mrs. Drew buys 12 apples. She buys 3 times as many oranges as apples. She also buys 3 times as many cherries as oranges. How many pieces of fruit does she buy altogether?

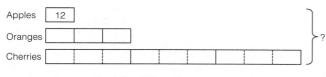

$$13 \times 12 = \mathbf{156}$$

6. The model that involves multiples and difference

There are 15 students in Class A. There are 5 more students in Class B than in Class A. There are 3 times as many students in Class C than in Class A. How many students are there altogether in the three classes?

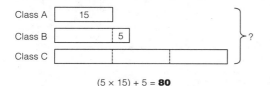

$$(5 \times 15) + 5 = \mathbf{80}$$

7. The model that involves creating a whole

Ellen, Giselle, and Brenda bake 111 muffins. Giselle bakes twice as many muffins as Brenda. Ellen bakes 9 fewer muffins than Giselle. How many muffins does Ellen bake?

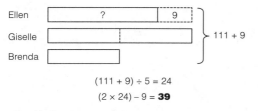

$$(111 + 9) \div 5 = 24$$
$$(2 \times 24) - 9 = \mathbf{39}$$

8. The model that involves sharing

There are 183 tennis balls in Basket A and 97 tennis balls in Basket B. How many tennis balls must be transferred from Basket A to Basket B so that both baskets contain the same number of tennis balls?

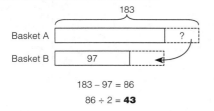

$$183 - 97 = 86$$
$$86 \div 2 = \mathbf{43}$$

9. The model that involves fractions

George had 355 marbles. He lost $\frac{1}{5}$ of the marbles and gave $\frac{1}{4}$ of the remaining marbles to his brother. How many marbles did he have left?

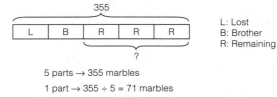

L: Lost
B: Brother
R: Remaining

5 parts → 355 marbles
1 part → 355 ÷ 5 = 71 marbles
3 parts → 3 × 71 = **213** marbles

10. The model that involves ratio

Aaron buys a tie and a belt. The prices of the tie and belt are in the ratio 2 : 5. If both items cost $539,

(a) what is the price of the tie?

(b) what is the price of the belt?

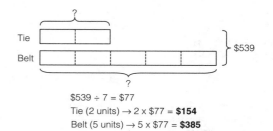

$$\$539 \div 7 = \$77$$
Tie (2 units) → 2 x $77 = **$154**
Belt (5 units) → 5 x $77 = **$385**

11. The model that involves comparison of fractions

Jack's height is $\frac{2}{3}$ of Leslie's height. Leslie's height is $\frac{3}{4}$ of Lindsay's height. If Lindsay is 160 cm tall, find Jack's height and Leslie's height.

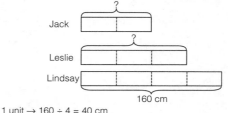

1 unit → 160 ÷ 4 = 40 cm

Leslie's height (3 units) → 3 × 40 = **120 cm**

Jack's height (2 units) → 2 × 40 = **80 cm**

Thinking skills and strategies are important in mathematical problem solving. These skills are applied when students think through the math problems to solve them. Below are some commonly used thinking skills and strategies applied in mathematical problem solving.

1. Comparing

Comparing is a form of thinking skill that students can apply to identify similarities and differences.

When comparing numbers, look carefully at each digit before deciding if a number is greater or less than the other. Students might also use a number line for comparison when there are more numbers.

Example:

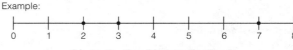

3 is greater than 2 but smaller than 7.

2. Sequencing

A sequence shows the order of a series of numbers. *Sequencing* is a form of thinking skill that requires students to place numbers in a particular order. There are many terms in a sequence. The terms refer to the numbers in a sequence.

To place numbers in a correct order, students must first find a rule that generates the sequence. In a simple math sequence, students can either add or subtract to find the unknown terms in the sequence.

Example: Find the 7th term in the sequence below.

1,	4,	7,	10,	13,	16	?
1st term	2nd term	3rd term	4th term	5th term	6th term	7th term

Step 1: This sequence is in an increasing order.

Step 2: 4 − 1 = 3   7 − 4 = 3
The difference between two consecutive terms is 3.

Step 3: 16 + 3 = 19
The 7th term is **19**.

3. Visualization

Visualization is a problem solving strategy that can help students visualize a problem through the use of physical objects. Students will play a more active role in solving the problem by manipulating these objects.

The main advantage of using this strategy is the mobility of information in the process of solving the problem. When students make a wrong step in the process, they can retrace the step without erasing or canceling it.

The other advantage is that this strategy helps develop a better understanding of the problem or solution through visual objects or images. In this way, students will be better able to remember how to solve these types of problems.

Some of the commonly used objects for this strategy are toothpicks, straws, cards, strings, water, sand, pencils, paper, and dice.

4. Look for a Pattern

This strategy requires the use of observational and analytical skills. Students have to observe the given data to find a pattern in order to solve the problem. Math word problems that involve the use of this strategy usually have repeated numbers or patterns.

Example: Find the sum of all the numbers from 1 to 100.

Step 1: <u>Simplify the problem.</u>
Find the sum of 1, 2, 3, 4, 5, 6, 7, 8, 9, and 10.

Step 2: <u>Look for a pattern.</u>

1 + 10 = 11	2 + 9 = 11	3 + 8 = 11
4 + 7 = 11	5 + 6 = 11	

Step 3: <u>Describe the pattern.</u>
When finding the sum of 1 to 10, add the first and last numbers to get a result of 11. Then, add the second and second last numbers to get the same result. The pattern continues until all the numbers from 1 to 10 are added. There will be 5 pairs of such results. Since each addition equals 11, the answer is then 5 × 11 = 55.

Step 4: <u>Use the pattern to find the answer.</u>
Since there are 5 pairs in the sum of 1 to 10, there should be (10 × 5 = 50 pairs) in the sum of 1 to 100.
Note that the addition for each pair is not equal to 11 now. The addition for each pair is now (1 + 100 = 101).
$$50 \times 101 = 5050$$
The sum of all the numbers from 1 to 100 is **5,050**.

5. Working Backward

The strategy of working backward applies only to a specific type of math word problem. These word problems state the end result, and students are required to find the total number. In order to solve these word problems, students have to work backward by thinking through the correct sequence of events. The strategy of working backward allows students to use their logical reasoning and sequencing to find the answers.

Example: Sarah has a piece of ribbon. She cuts the ribbon into 4 equal parts. Each part is then cut into 3 smaller equal parts. If the length of each small part is 35 cm, how long is the piece of ribbon?
$$3 \times 35 = 105 \text{ cm}$$
$$4 \times 105 = 420 \text{ cm}$$
The piece of ribbon is **420 cm**.

6. The Before-After Concept

The *Before-After* concept lists all the relevant data before and after an event. Students can then compare the differences and eventually solve the problems. Usually, the Before-After concept and the mathematical model go hand in hand to solve math word problems. Note that the Before-After concept can be applied only to a certain type of math word problem, which trains students to think sequentially.

Example: Kelly has 4 times as much money as Joey. After Kelly uses some money to buy a tennis racquet, and Joey uses $30 to buy a pair of pants, Kelly has twice as much money as Joey. If Joey has $98 in the beginning,
(a) how much money does Kelly have in the end?
(b) how much money does Kelly spend on the tennis racquet?

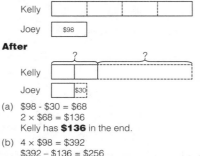

(a) $98 - $30 = $68
2 × $68 = $136
Kelly has **$136** in the end.
(b) 4 × $98 = $392
$392 – $136 = $256
Kelly spends **$256** on the tennis racquet.

7. Making Supposition

Making supposition is commonly known as "making an assumption." Students can use this strategy to solve certain types of math word problems. Making

assumptions will eliminate some possibilities and simplifies the word problems by providing a boundary of values to work within.

Example: Mrs. Jackson bought 100 pieces of candy for all the students in her class. How many pieces of candy would each student receive if there were 25 students in her class?

In the above word problem, assume that each student received the same number of pieces. This eliminates the possibilities that some students would receive more than others due to good behaviour, better results, or any other reason.

8. Representation of Problem

In problem solving, students often use representations in the solutions to show their understanding of the problems. Using representations also allow students to understand the mathematical concepts and relationships as well as to manipulate the information presented in the problems. Examples of representations are diagrams and lists or tables.

Diagrams allow students to consolidate or organize the information given in the problems. By drawing a diagram, students can see the problem clearly and solve it effectively.

A list or table can help students organize information that is useful for analysis. After analyzing, students can then see a pattern, which can be used to solve the problem.

9. Guess and Check

One of the most important and effective problem-solving techniques is *Guess and Check*. It is also known as *Trial and Error*. As the name suggests, students have to guess the answer to a problem and check if that guess is correct. If the guess is wrong, students will make another guess. This will continue until the guess is correct.

It is beneficial to keep a record of all the guesses and checks in a table. In addition, a *Comments* column can be included. This will enable students to analyze their guess (if it is too high or too low) and improve on the next guess. Be careful; this problem-solving technique can be tiresome without systematic or logical guesses.

Example: Jessica had 15 coins. Some of them were 10-cent coins and the rest were 5-cent coins. The total amount added up to $1.25. How many coins of each kind were there?

Use the guess-and-check method.

Number of 10¢ Coins	Value	Number of 5¢ Coins	Value	Total Number of Coins	Total Value
7	7 × 10¢ = 70¢	8	8 × 5¢ = 40¢	7 + 8 = 15	70¢ + 40¢ = 110¢ = $1.10
8	8 × 10¢ = 80¢	7	7 × 5¢ = 35¢	8 + 7 = 15	80¢ + 35¢ = 115¢ = $1.15
10	10 × 10¢ = 100¢	5	5 × 5¢ = 25¢	10 + 5 = 15	100¢ + 25¢ = 125¢ = $1.25

There were **ten** 10-cent coins and **five** 5-cent coins.

10. Restate the Problem

When solving challenging math problems, conventional methods may not be workable. Instead, restating the problem will enable students to see some challenging problems in a different light so that they can better understand them.

The strategy of restating the problem is to "say" the problem in a different and clearer way. However, students have to ensure that the main idea of the problem is not altered.

How do students restate a math problem?

First, read and understand the problem. Gather the given facts and unknowns. Note any condition(s) that have to be satisfied.

Next, restate the problem. Imagine narrating this problem to a friend. Present the given facts, unknown(s), and condition(s). Students may want to write the "revised" problem. Once the "revised" problem is analyzed, students should be able to think of an appropriate strategy to solve it.

11. Simplify the Problem

One of the commonly used strategies in mathematical problem solving is simplification of the problem. When a problem is simplified, it can be "broken down" into two or more smaller parts. Students can then solve the parts systematically to get to the final answer.

Table of Contents

Word Problems

1-70

Question 3

Olivia has 19 stamps. She gives 16 stamps to her brother. How many stamps does she have now?

$$\boxed{19} \; \bigcirc \; \boxed{16} = \boxed{1\varepsilon}$$

She has (1ε) stamps now.

Maddy has 8 dolls. Amira has 4 dolls more than her. How many dolls does Amira have?

$$\boxed{8} \;\; \oplus \;\; \boxed{4} \; = \; \boxed{12}$$

Amira has ⌈ 12 ⌋ dolls.

Question 5

James has 13 toy boats. Henry has 6 toy boats. How many fewer toy boats does Henry have than James?

$$\boxed{13} \enspace \bigcirc \enspace \boxed{5} = \boxed{6}$$

Henry has $\boxed{5}$ fewer toy boats than James.

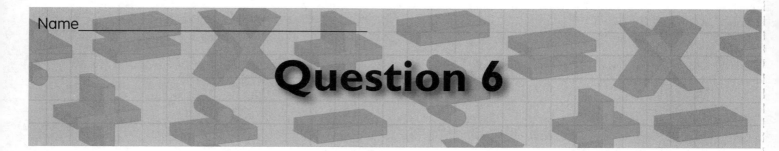

Question 6

8 ducks are swimming in a lake. 4 more ducks join them. How many ducks are swimming in the lake now?

There are (12) ducks swimming in the lake now.

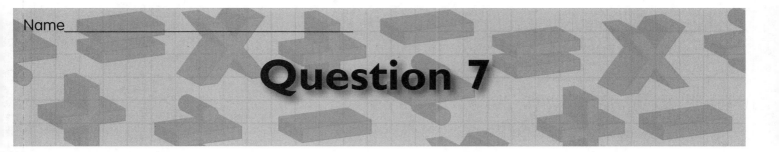
Michael had 14 pieces of cake. He ate 3 pieces of cake. How many pieces were left?

$$\boxed{14} \;\bigcirc\!\!-\!\!\bigcirc\; \boxed{3} = \boxed{11}$$

He had (11) pieces of cake left.

Kenji had some pens. He kept 3 pens for himself and gave the remaining 8 pens to his friends. How many pens did he have in the beginning?

He had [   ] pens in the beginning.

Mrs. Jackson needs 9 eggs to bake 6 cakes. She has only 4 eggs. How many more eggs does she need to bake the cakes?

She needs ⬭ more eggs to bake the cakes.

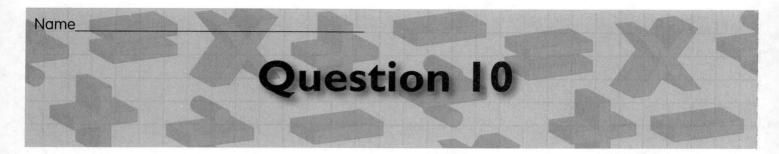
Jasmine has 6 books. Drew has 3 books. How many books do they have altogether?

$$\boxed{} \bigcirc \boxed{} = \boxed{}$$

They have $\boxed{}$ books altogether.

There are 8 pink golf balls and 7 white golf balls on the golf course. How many golf balls are there altogether?

There are ⬭ golf balls altogether.

Hannah has 8 pieces of candy. Her mother gives her 4 more pieces. How many pieces of candy does Hannah have now?

Hannah has [   ] pieces of candy now.

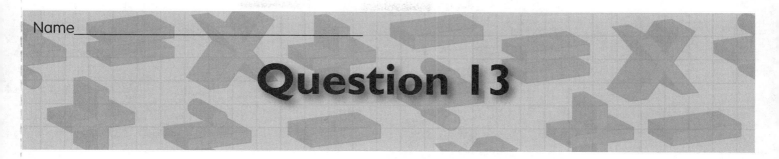

Question 13

Ahmad has 7 marbles. Kate has 4 marbles more than him. How many marbles does Kate have?

Kate has ⌐────────⌐ marbles.

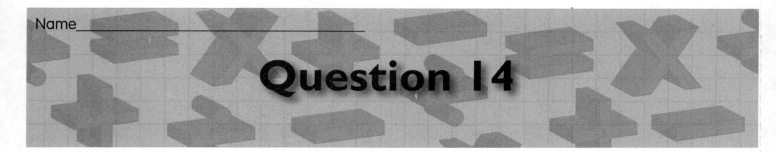

Angelo gave 7 stamps to Dante. He has 8 stamps left. How many stamps did Angelo have in the beginning?

$$\boxed{} \bigcirc \boxed{} = \boxed{}$$

Angelo had ⬭ stamps in the beginning.

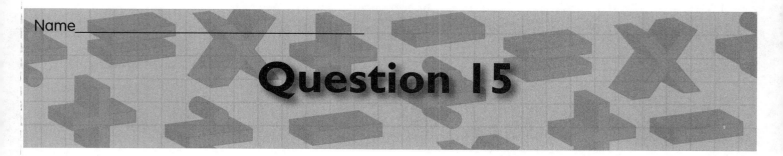
Braden has 6 stickers. Michael has 7 stickers more than him. How many stickers does Michael have?

$$\boxed{} \bigcirc \boxed{} = \boxed{}$$

Michael has $\boxed{}$ stickers.

Aisha has 2 dolls. Sarah has 3 dolls more than her.

(a)   How many dolls does Sarah have?

(b)   How many dolls do they have altogether?

(a)

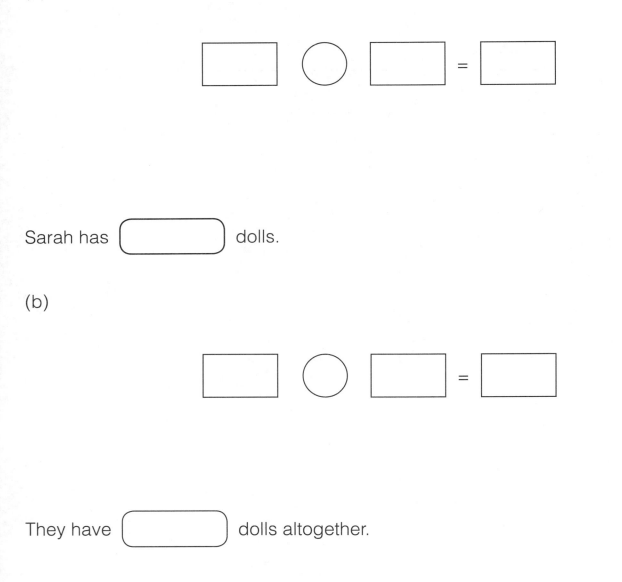

Sarah has ⬚ dolls.

(b)

They have ⬚ dolls altogether.

Question 17

Dad gives Cody 7 pens. Dad gives Dominic 4 pens.

(a)   How many pens does Dad give to the two boys?

(b)   How many more pens does Cody have than Dominic?

(a)

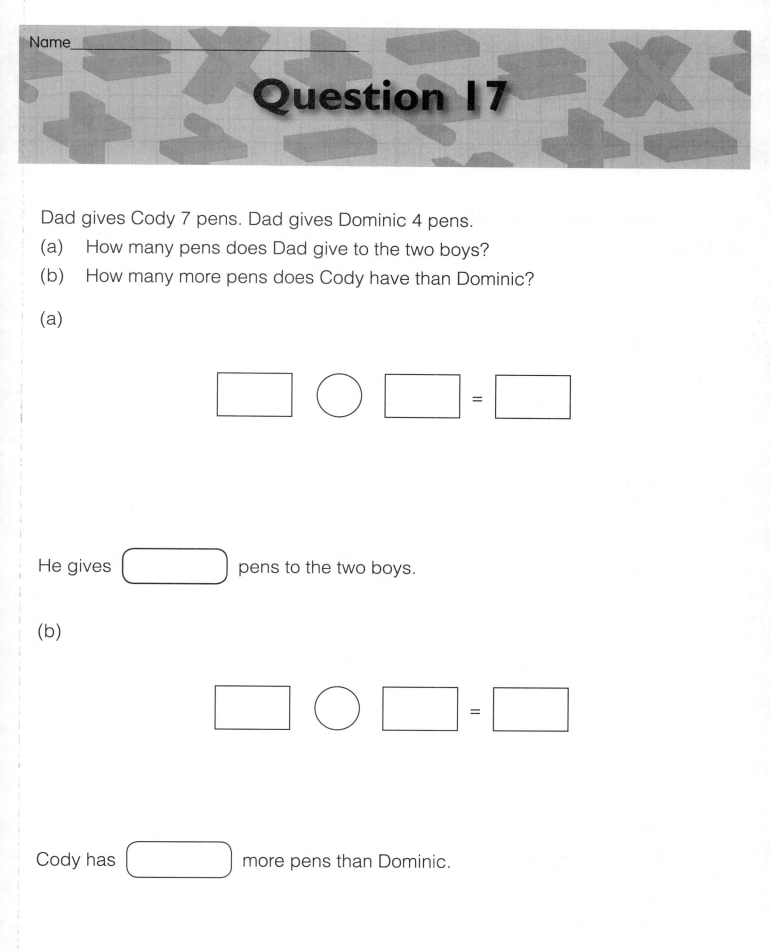

He gives [   ] pens to the two boys.

(b)

Cody has [   ] more pens than Dominic.

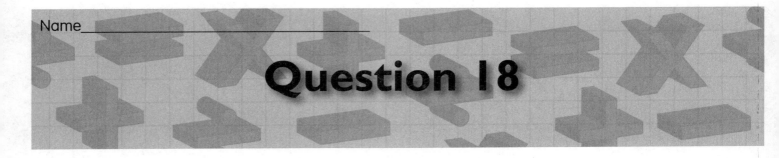
Emma has 4 more cakes than Riley. If Emma has 9 cakes, how many cakes does Riley have?

Riley has ⬚ cakes.

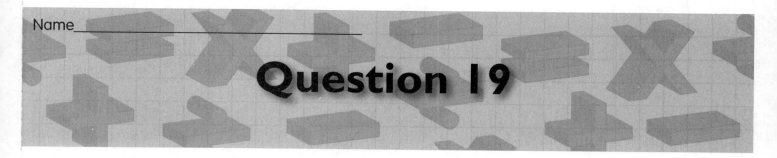

Question 19

At the market, Mr. Chen sold 8 baskets of oranges on Monday, 6 baskets of oranges on Tuesday, and 4 baskets of oranges on Wednesday. How many baskets of oranges did Mr. Chen sell altogether?

$$\boxed{} \bigcirc \boxed{} \bigcirc \boxed{} = \boxed{}$$

Mr. Chen sold $\boxed{}$ baskets of oranges altogether.

Question 20

David has 8 fewer stamps than Elena. If Elena has 19 stamps, how many stamps does David have?

David has ⬚ stamps.

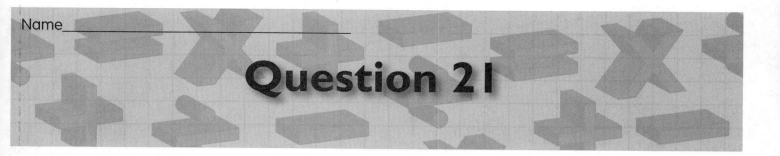

Question 21

Jessica has 14 coins. Kyoko has 8 coins. How many fewer coins does Kyoko have than Jessica?

Kyoko has [   ] fewer coins than Jessica.

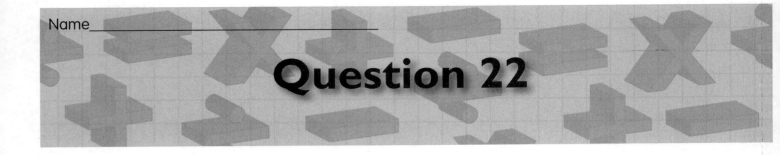

Jane has 8 books. Ethan has 5 books more than her. How many books does Ethan have?

Ethan has ⬭ books.

Question 23

Mrs. Drew baked 9 cakes on Saturday and 11 cakes on Sunday.

(a) How many cakes did Mrs. Drew bake altogether?

(b) She gave 4 cakes to her neighbor and the rest to her children. How many cakes did she give to her children?

(a)

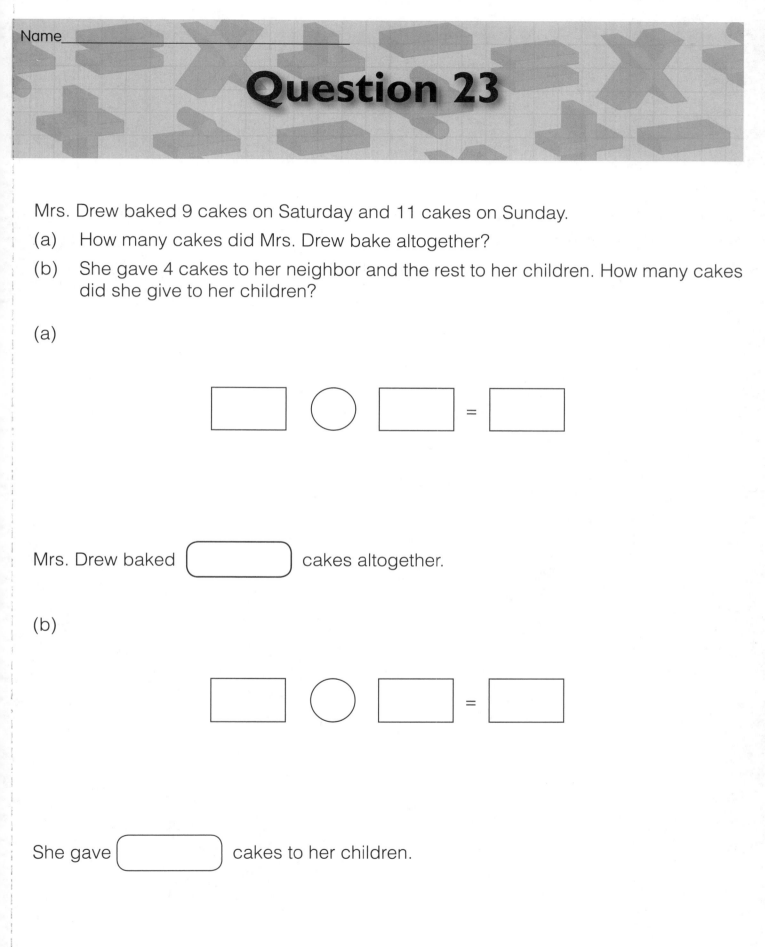

Mrs. Drew baked [   ] cakes altogether.

(b)

She gave [   ] cakes to her children.

Question 24

Andy scored 9 points on his math test. Omar scored 3 points less than him.

(a)   How many points did Omar score?

(b)   How many points did they score altogether?

(a)

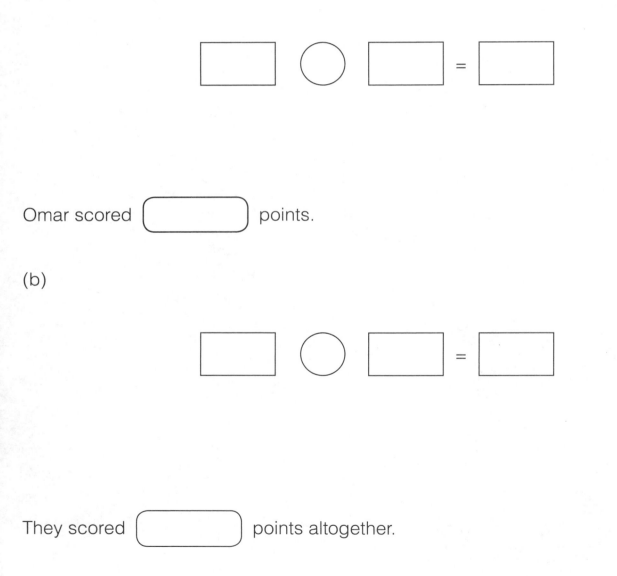

Omar scored ⬭ points.

(b)

They scored ⬭ points altogether.

Question 25

Alex likes to eat apples. If Alex eats an apple a day for 7 days, how many apples does Alex eat in a week?

☐ ○ ☐ = ☐

Alex eats ☐ apples in a week.

Nate is 15 years old. Jackson is 3 years older than Nate. How old is Jackson?

$$\boxed{} \bigcirc \boxed{} = \boxed{}$$

Jackson is $\boxed{}$ years old.

Question 27

Aliyah has 16 goldfish. Isabel has 7 goldfish. How many more goldfish does Aliyah have than Isabel?

Aliyah has [   ] more goldfish than Isabel.

There are 14 kiwifruits in a basket. Mr. Goldberg puts 5 more kiwis into the basket. How many kiwis are in the basket now?

There are [ ] kiwis in the basket now.

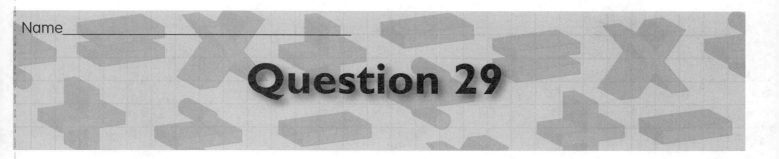

Question 29

There are 18 students in a classroom. 6 of them are girls. How many boys are there?

$$\boxed{} \bigcirc \boxed{} = \boxed{}$$

There are $\boxed{}$ boys.

Diego has 19 pencils. He gives 4 pencils to Jin. How many pencils does Diego have left?

Diego has ⬭ pencils left.

Peter has 9 cards. Benny has 4 more cards than him. How many cards does Benny have?

Benny has ⬭ cards.

There are 13 chickens and 4 ducks on a farm. How many more chickens than ducks are there?

There are [   ] more chickens than ducks.

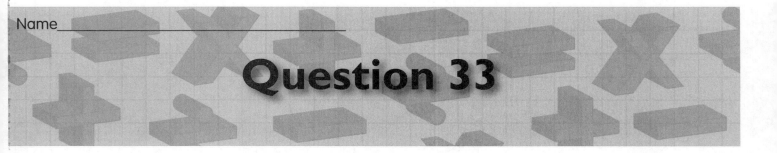

There are 14 boys in the music room. There are 5 more girls than boys. How many girls are in the music room?

There are ⬭ girls in the music room.

Lily has 16 stamps. She has 3 stamps fewer than Andre. How many stamps does Andre have?

Andre has [   ] stamps.

Question 35

There are 19 adults on a train. 7 of them are women. The rest are men. How many men are on the train?

There are [   ] men on the train.

Deepak collected 17 ice-cream sticks. How many more must he collect in order to have 20 ice-cream sticks?

He must collect ⬚ more ice-cream sticks.

Question 37

Sophia has 5 blue bows. Trina gives Sophia 6 pink bows. Abby gives Sophia 4 red bows. How many bows does Sophia have altogether?

☐ ◯ ☐ ◯ ☐ = ☐

Sophia has ⬭ bows altogether.

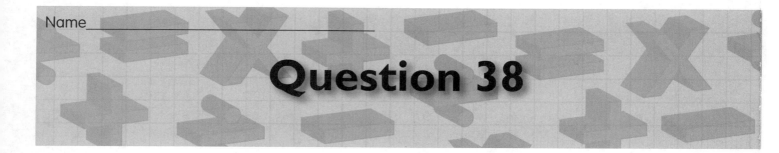

Akiko's babysitter is 20 years old. Akiko is 8 years old. How much older is her babysitter than Akiko?

Akiko's babysitter is [   ] years older than Akiko.

Mom bought 7 boxes of crackers. There were 3 crackers in each box. How many crackers did she buy in all?

She bought ⬭ crackers in all.

There are 19 boys on Bus A. There are 8 boys on Bus B. How many more boys are on Bus A than on Bus B?

There are [____] more boys on Bus A than on Bus B.

In a music class of 20 students, 5 students were absent. How many students came to class?

$$\boxed{} \bigcirc \boxed{} = \boxed{}$$

$\boxed{}$ students came to class.

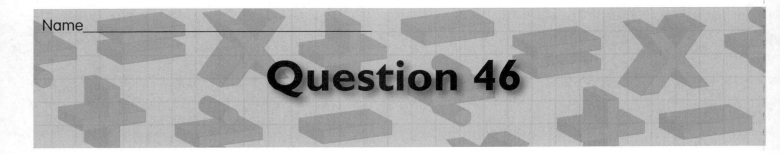

Grace has 4 baskets. She puts 5 oranges in each basket. How many oranges does she have in all?

She has ⬭ oranges in all.

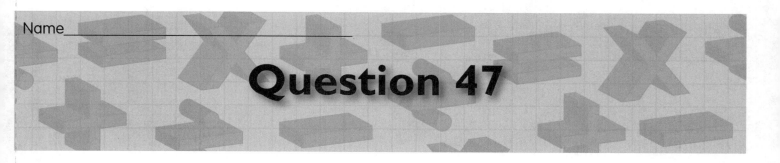
Lela needs 15 sacks of flour to bake 10 cakes. She has 9 sacks of flour now. How many more sacks of flour does she need?

She needs [   ] more sacks of flour.

Kenny has 8 fewer erasers than Marcus. If Marcus has 16 erasers, how many erasers does Kenny have?

Kenny has ⬭ erasers.

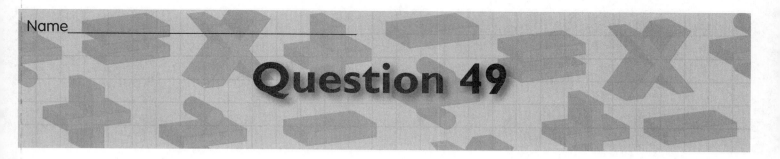

Question 49

After eating 9 pieces of candy, John had 13 pieces left. How many pieces did he have in the beginning?

He had [   ] pieces of candy in the beginning.

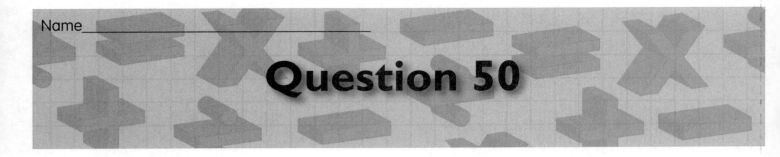

Question 50

There are as many girls as boys at a library. If there are 9 girls, how many children are there altogether?

There are [   ] children altogether.

Name_____

Question 51

Eva has 15 books on her bookshelf. 9 of them are Spanish books and the rest are English. How many English books are there?

$$\boxed{} \bigcirc \boxed{} = \boxed{}$$

There are ⬭ English books.

Name_____

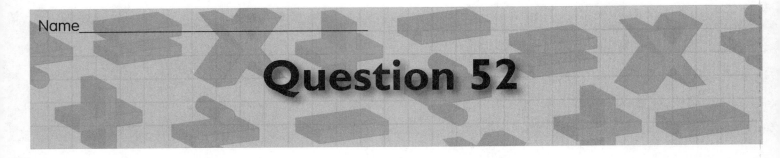

Billy has 20 toy cars. Terrell has 9 toy cars. How many toy cars do they have altogether?

They have [   ] toy cars altogether.

Asia has 19 stamps. She shares them with her brother and sister. She keeps 7 stamps for herself. How many stamps does she share with her brother and sister?

She shares [ ] stamps with her brother and sister.

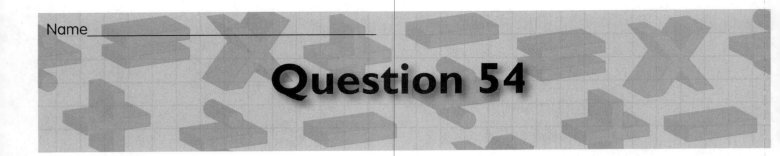

Mrs. Patel has 6 plates. She puts 5 pieces of cake on each plate. How many pieces of cake are there altogether?

There are [   ] pieces of cake altogether.

Mr. Delaney had 18 watermelons. He sold 9 of them. How many watermelons were left?

He had $\boxed{}$ watermelons left.

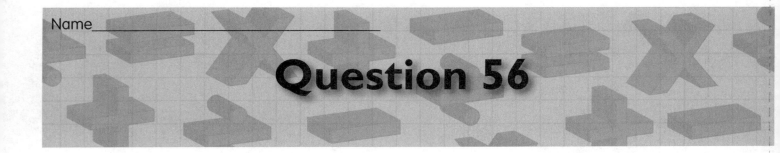
Mei had 17 buttons. She used 4 buttons. How many buttons did Mei have left?

☐ ◯ ☐ = ☐

Mei had ☐ buttons left.

Question 57

Colin and Anna have 40 stickers altogether. Anna has 16 stickers.

(a)   How many stickers does Colin have?

(b)   If Colin gives 9 stickers to Anna, how many stickers does he have now?

(a)

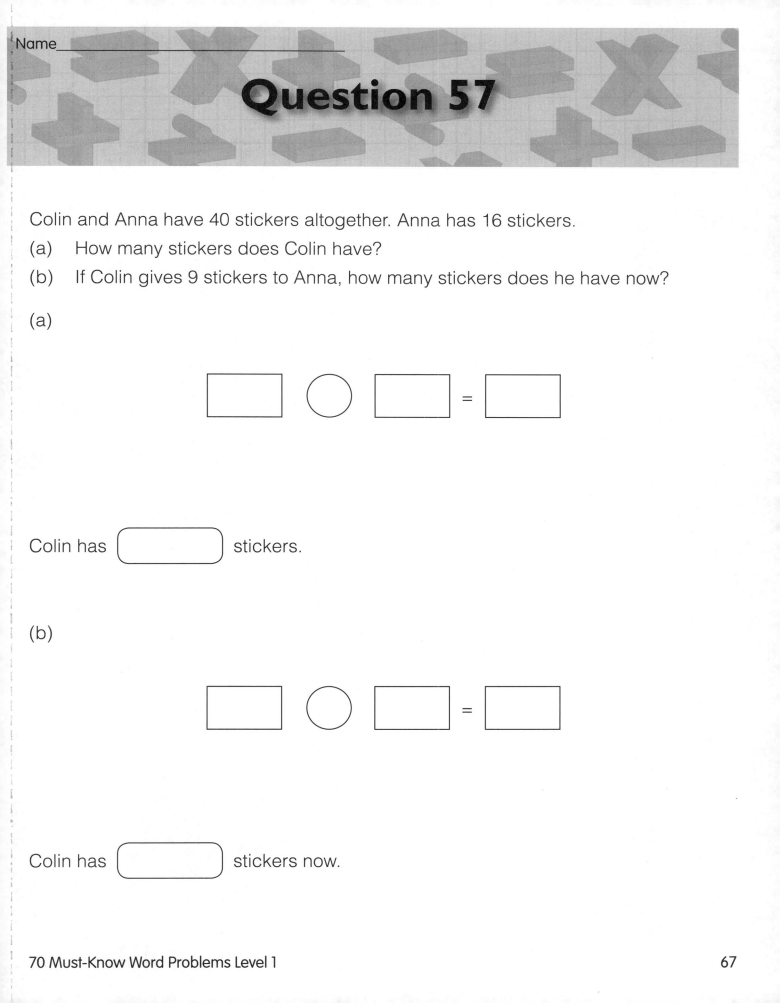

Colin has (_____) stickers.

(b)

Colin has (_____) stickers now.

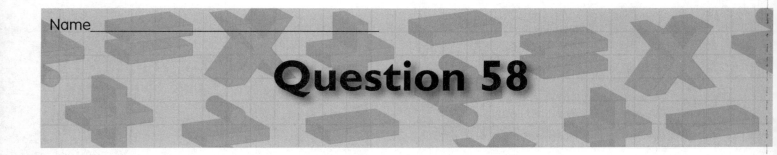

Question 58

There are 5 children in each group. How many children are there in 3 groups?

There are [   ] children in 3 groups.

There are 4 groups of boys. How many boys are there altogether if there are 6 boys in each group?

There are ⬭ boys altogether.

Jacob is 8 years old. His mother is 4 times his age. How old is his mother?

$$\boxed{} \bigcirc \boxed{} = \boxed{}$$

His mother is $\boxed{}$ years old.

Question 61

Zoe had some coins. Her father gave her 15 more coins. She has 40 coins now. How many coins did she have in the beginning?

She had ⬭ coins in the beginning.

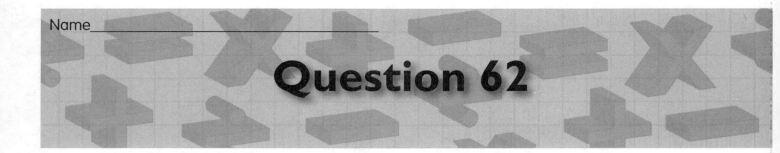

There are 6 cars parked in a parking lot. Each car has 4 wheels. How many wheels are there altogether?

There are ⬭ wheels altogether.

There are 7 vases on the table. Mrs. Klaus puts 4 roses into each vase. How many roses are there altogether?

There are ⬭ roses altogether.

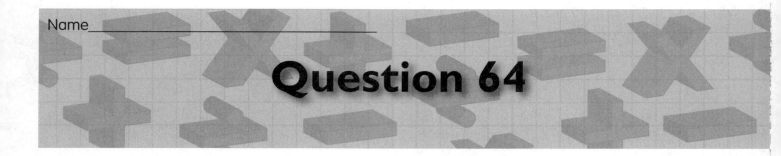
Luke, Tomas, and Maya bought 6 movie tickets each. How many movie tickets did they buy in all?

They bought ⬭ movie tickets in all.

Hailey buys 5 bags of candy. There are 7 pieces of candy in each bag. How many pieces of candy are there altogether?

There are ⬭ pieces of candy altogether.

A T-shirt costs $18, and a pair of shoes costs $28. How much more does the pair of shoes cost than the T-shirt?

$ [＿＿＿] ◯ $ [＿＿＿] = $ [＿＿＿]

The pair of shoes costs $ (＿＿＿) more than the T-shirt.

Question 67

Mrs. Wright bakes 20 cookies. She puts 4 cookies on each plate. How many plates does she need?

She needs ( ) plates.

A pencil costs 50 cents. A pen costs 90 cents. How much cheaper is the pencil?

The pencil is ⬭ cents cheaper.

Question 69

Mrs. Guzman bought 16 strawberries. She shared them equally among her 4 children. How many strawberries did each child get?

Each child got ( ) strawberries.

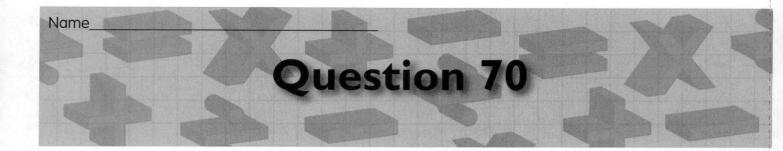
Alyssa shared 12 beads equally with Connor, Julio, and Ling. How many beads did each child get?

Each child got ⬭ beads.

Solutions to Word Problems 1-70

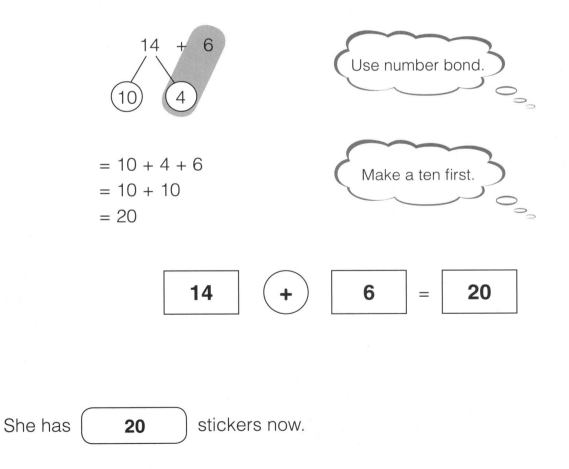

14 + 6

10   4

Use number bond.

= 10 + 4 + 6
= 10 + 10
= 20

Make a ten first.

| 14 | (+) | 6 | = | 20 |

She has [**20**] stickers now.

Solution to Question 2

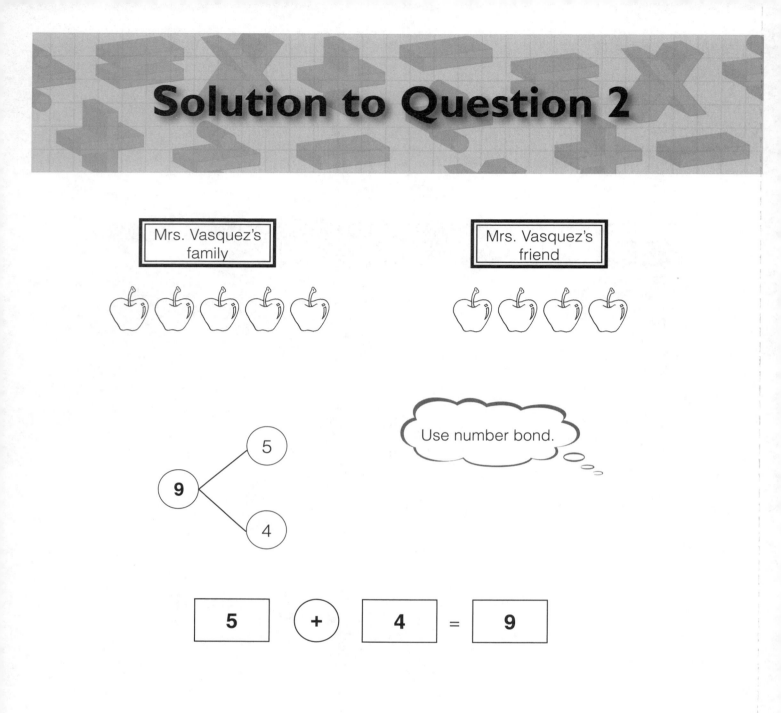

| Mrs. Vasquez's family | | Mrs. Vasquez's friend |

5

9

4

Use number bond.

| 5 | + | 4 | = | 9 |

She bought [9] apples in the beginning.

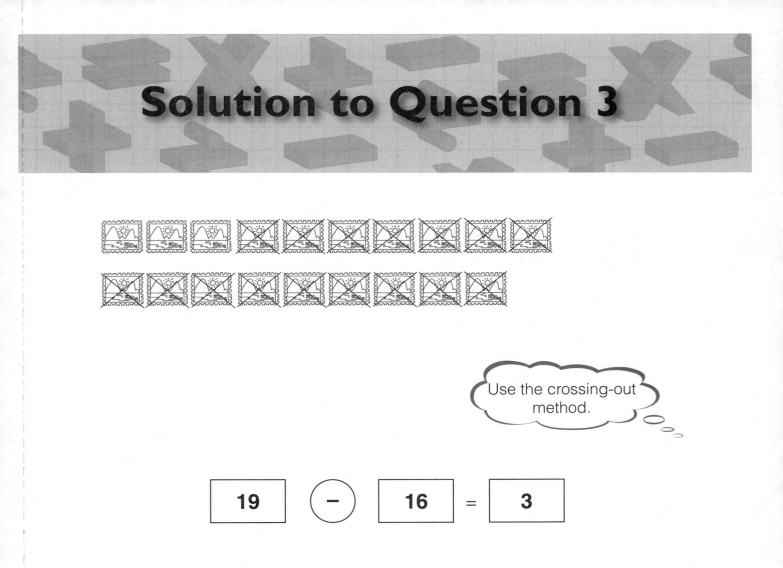

Use the crossing-out method.

19 − 16 = 3

She has 3 stamps now.

Solution to Question 4

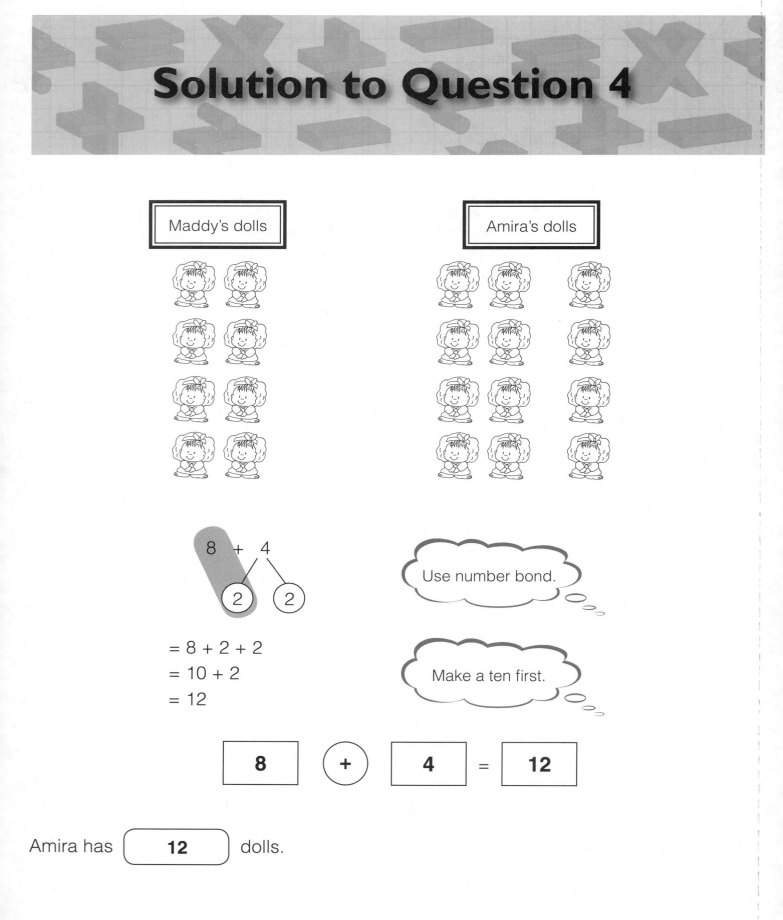

Maddy's dolls

Amira's dolls

8 + 4
2   2

= 8 + 2 + 2
= 10 + 2
= 12

Use number bond.

Make a ten first.

| 8 | + | 4 | = | 12 |

Amira has   12   dolls.

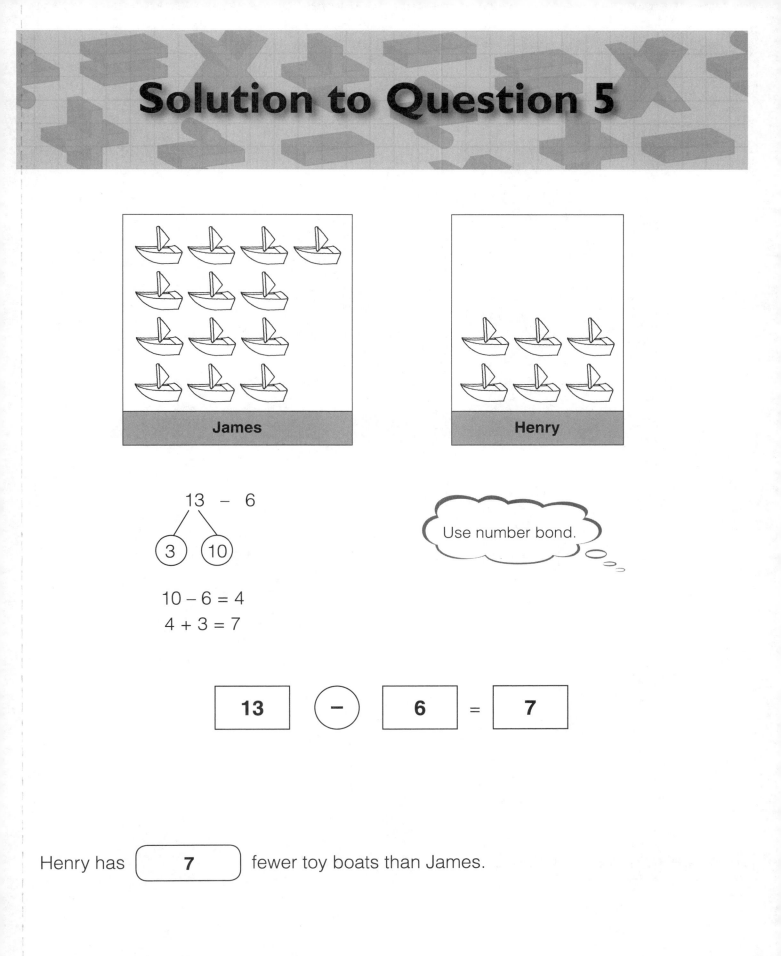

James

Henry

13 – 6

3   10

10 − 6 = 4
4 + 3 = 7

Use number bond.

13 ⊖ 6 = 7

Henry has 7 fewer toy boats than James.

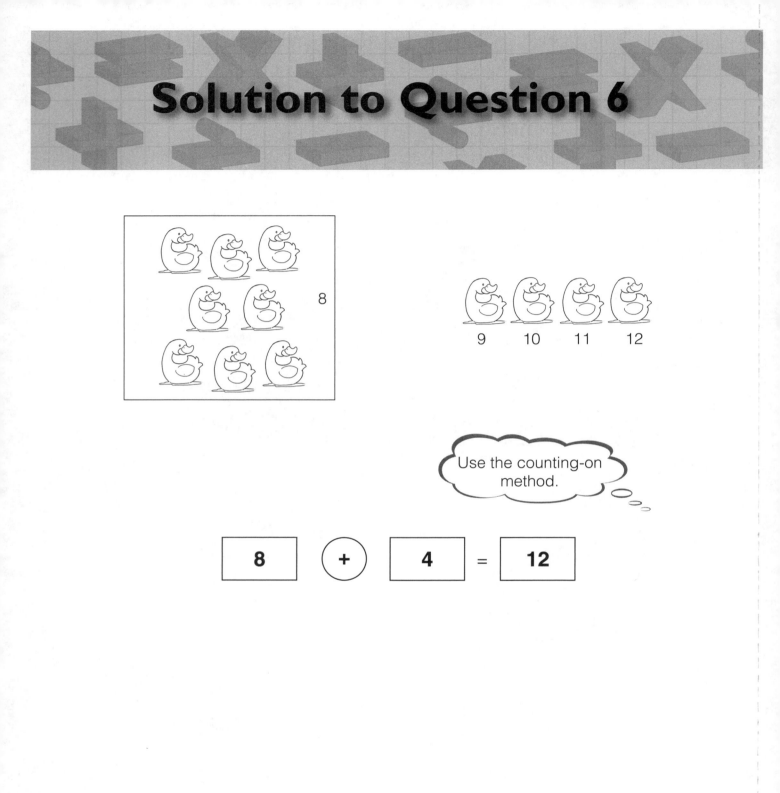

8

9   10   11   12

Use the counting-on method.

| 8 | $+$ | 4 | = | 12 |

There are   12   ducks swimming in the lake now.

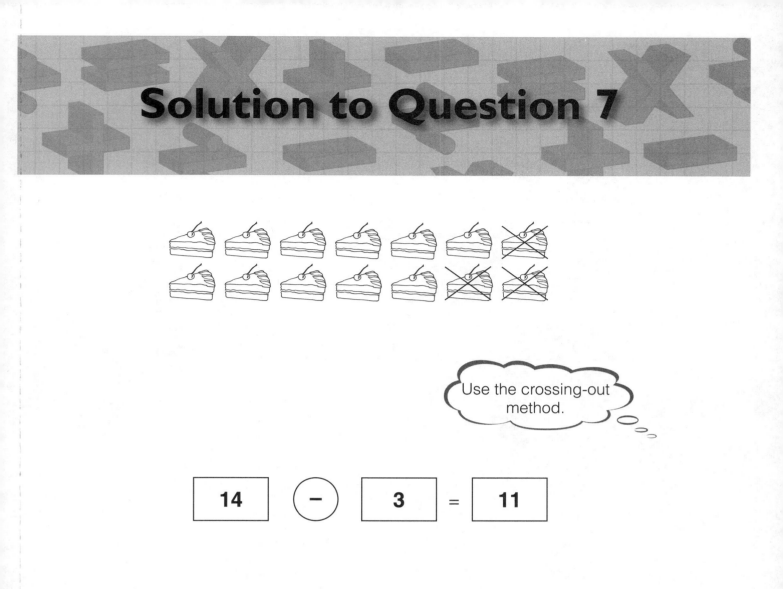

14 − 3 = 11

He had ⟨ 11 ⟩ pieces of cake left.

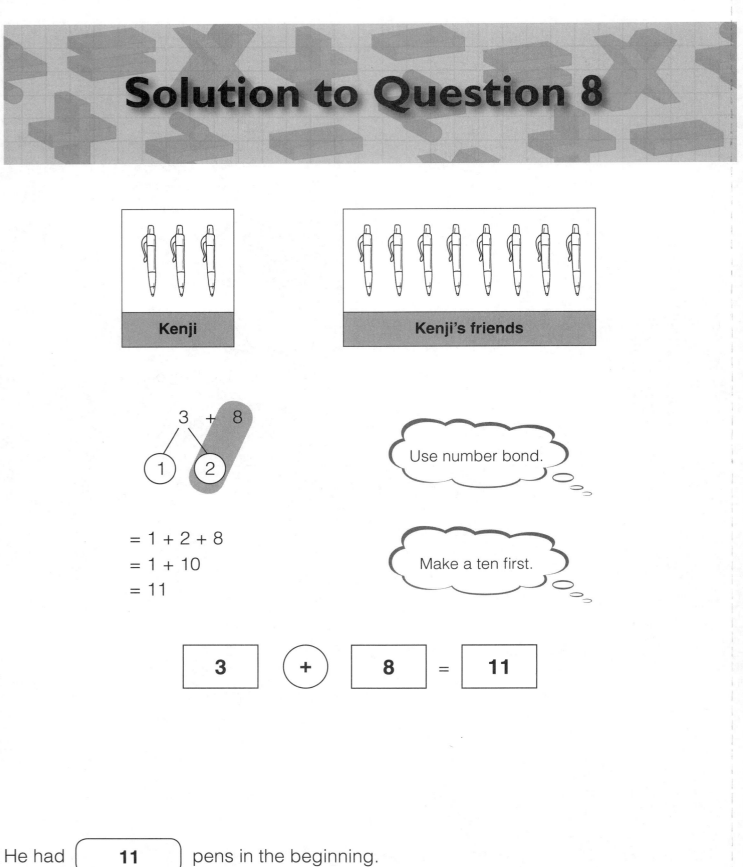

Kenji

Kenji's friends

3 + 8

1   2

Use number bond.

= 1 + 2 + 8
= 1 + 10
= 11

Make a ten first.

| **3** | **+** | **8** | **=** | **11** |

He had (**11**) pens in the beginning.

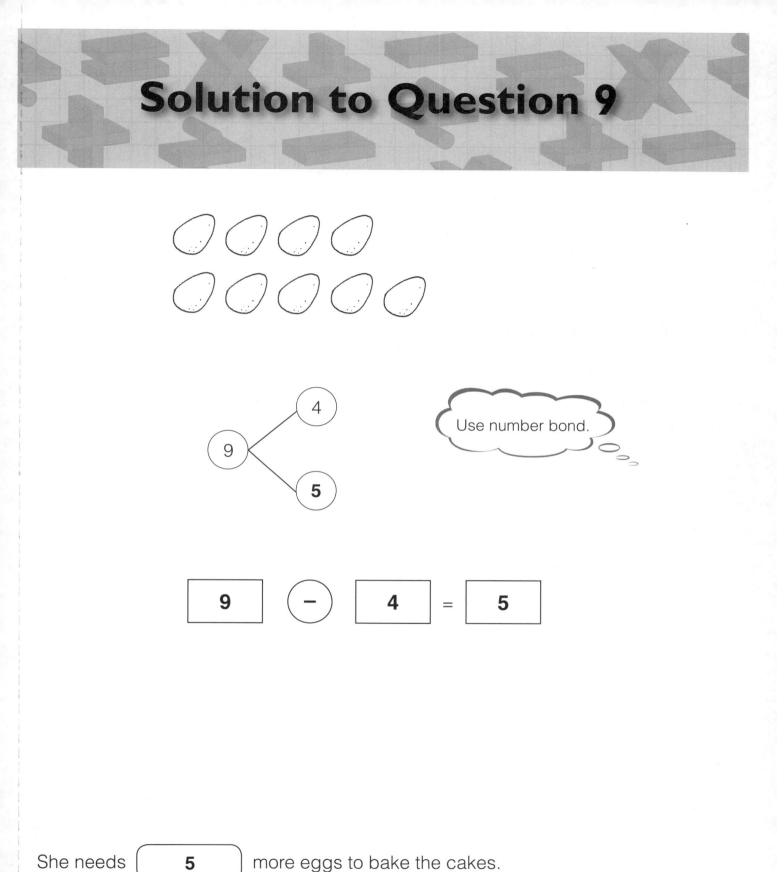

Use number bond.

9 — 4 = 5

She needs [5] more eggs to bake the cakes.

Solution to Question 10

| Jasmine's books | | Drew's books |

```
        6
       /
   9
       \
        3
```

Use number bond.

| 6 | (+) | 3 | = | 9 |

They have [**9**] books altogether.

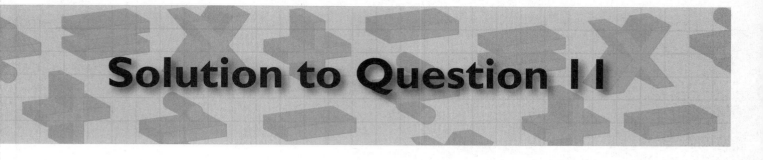

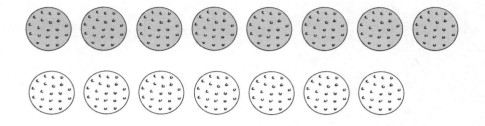

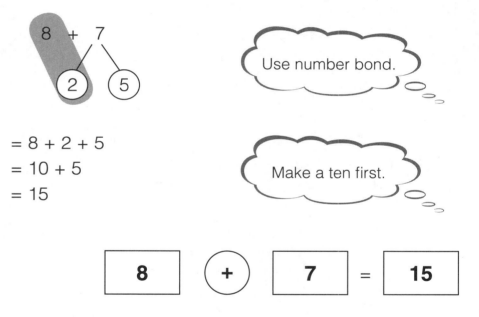

= 8 + 2 + 5
= 10 + 5
= 15

Use number bond.

Make a ten first.

| 8 | + | 7 | = | 15 |

There are [15] golf balls altogether.

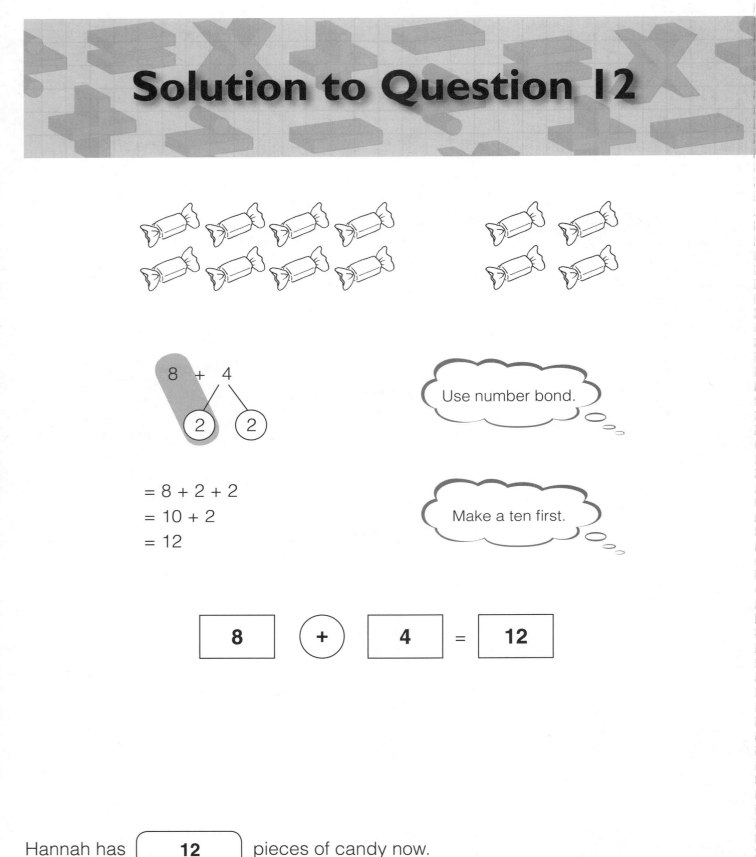

= 8 + 2 + 2
= 10 + 2
= 12

Use number bond.

Make a ten first.

8 (+) 4 = 12

Hannah has [**12**] pieces of candy now.

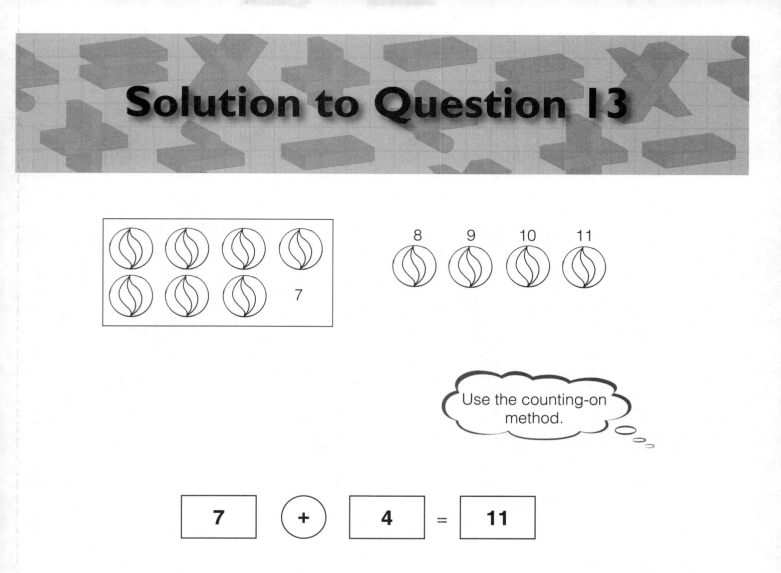

$$\boxed{7} \; \bigoplus \; \boxed{4} \; = \; \boxed{11}$$

Kate has $\boxed{11}$ marbles.

Solution to Question 14

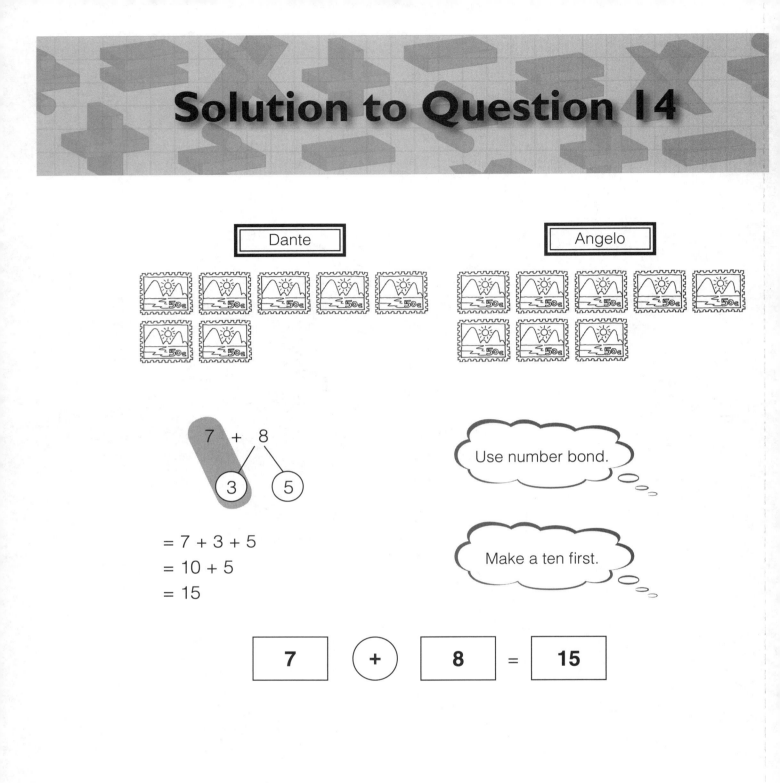

Dante

Angelo

7 + 8

3   5

= 7 + 3 + 5
= 10 + 5
= 15

Use number bond.

Make a ten first.

| 7 | (+) | 8 | = | 15 |

Angelo had 15 stamps in the beginning.

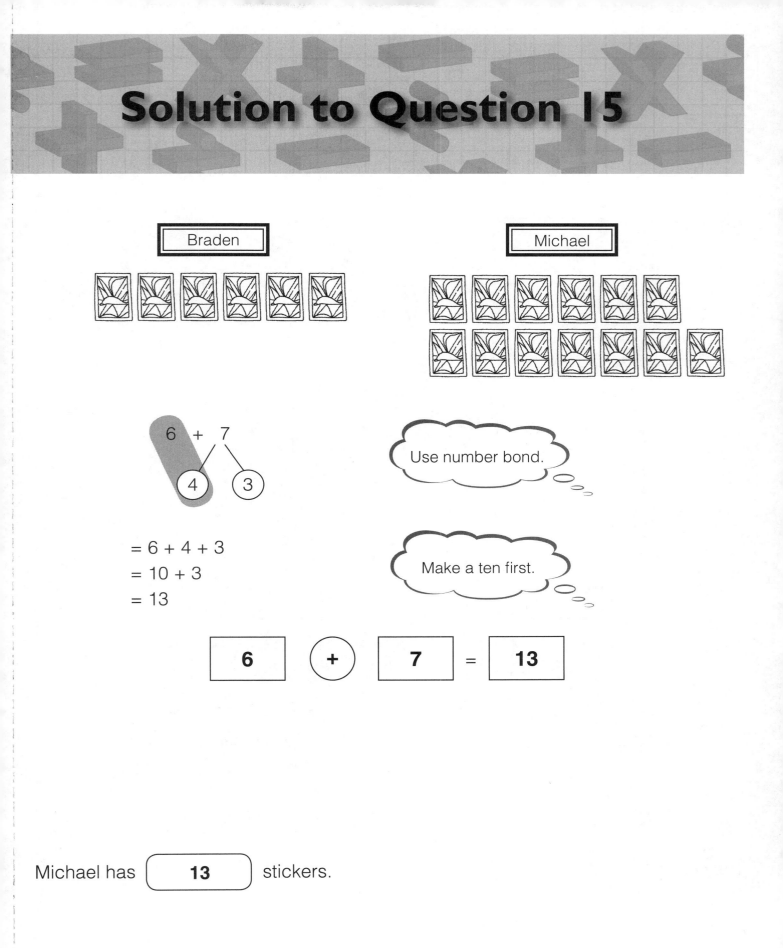

Braden

Michael

$6 + 7$

$4 \quad 3$

$= 6 + 4 + 3$
$= 10 + 3$
$= 13$

Use number bond.

Make a ten first.

| 6 | + | 7 | = | 13 |

Michael has 13 stickers.

Solution to Question 16

(a)

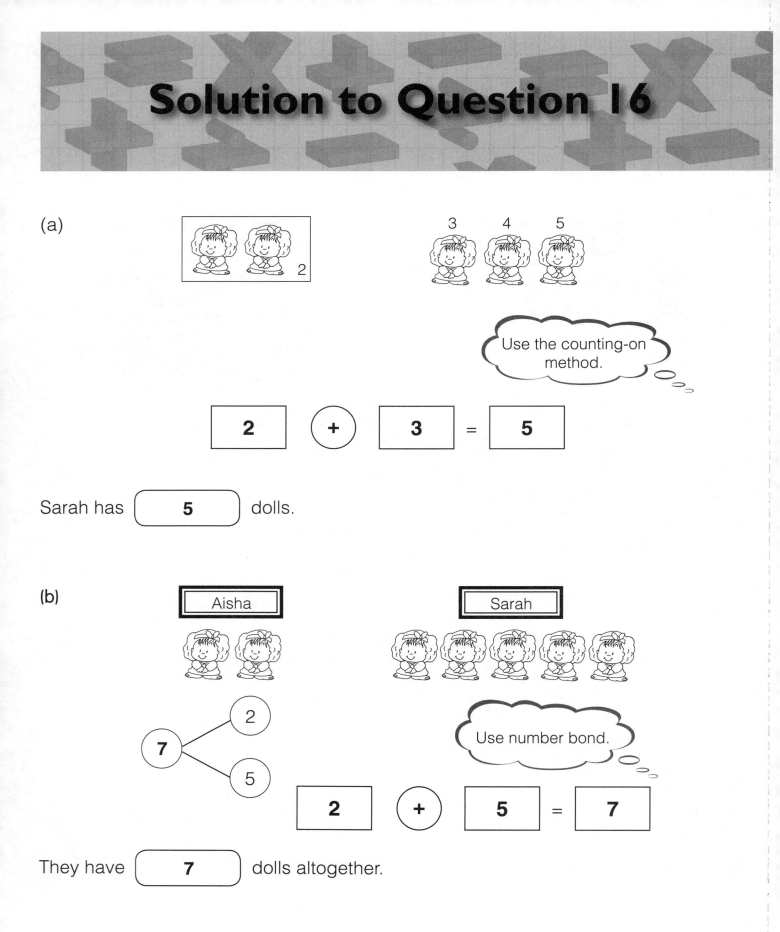

3 4 5

Use the counting-on method.

| 2 | + | 3 | = | 5 |

Sarah has [5] dolls.

(b)

Aisha   Sarah

Use number bond.

7 — 2
    5

| 2 | + | 5 | = | 7 |

They have [7] dolls altogether.

(a)

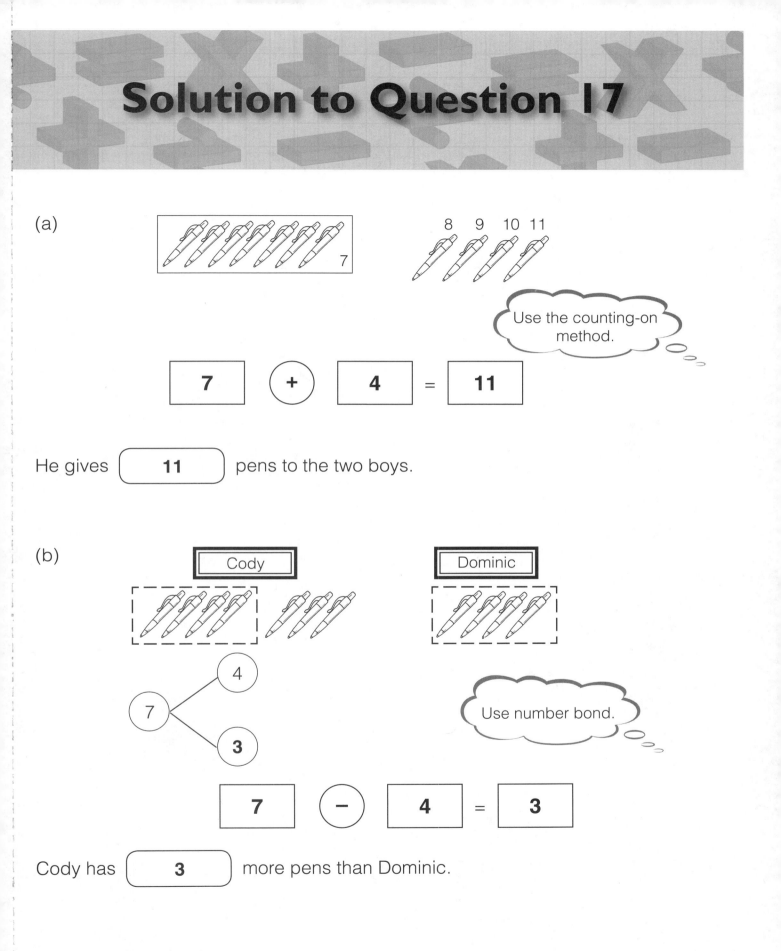

8 9 10 11

Use the counting-on method.

| 7 | + | 4 | = | 11 |

He gives [11] pens to the two boys.

(b)

Cody

Dominic

7
4
3

Use number bond.

| 7 | − | 4 | = | 3 |

Cody has [3] more pens than Dominic.

Solution to Question 18

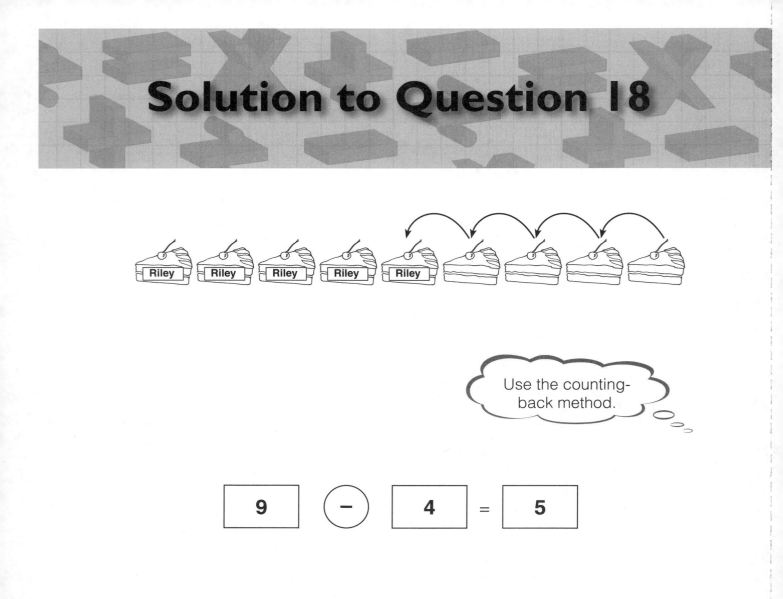

Use the counting-back method.

$$9 \; - \; 4 \; = \; 5$$

Riley has **5** cakes.

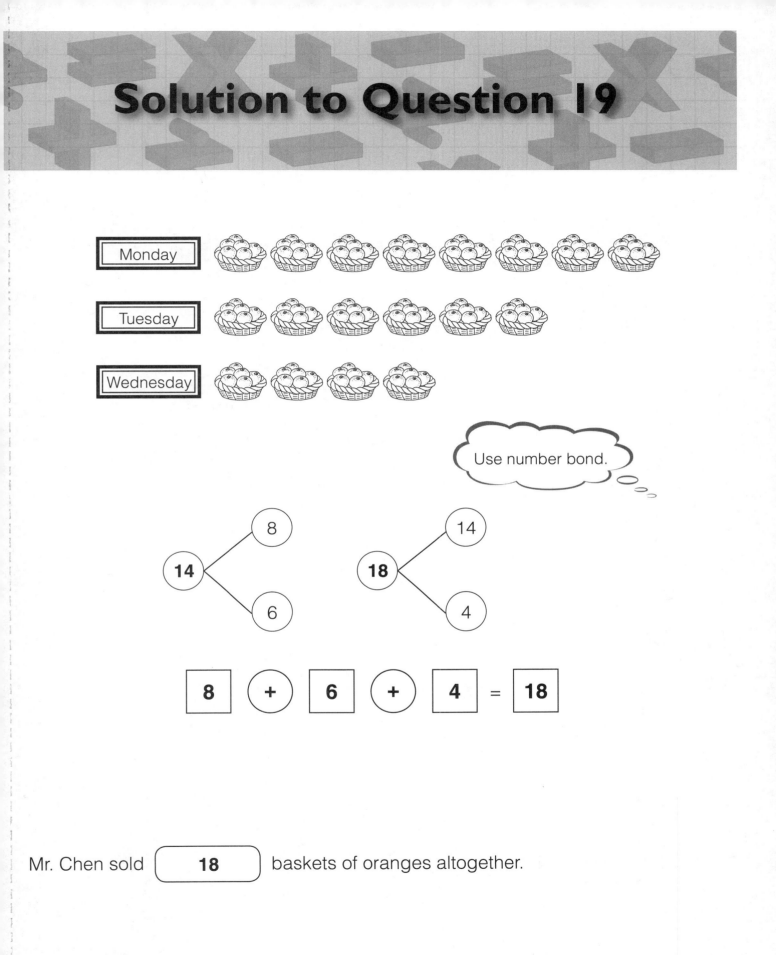

Monday

Tuesday

Wednesday

Use number bond.

8 + 6 + 4 = 18

Mr. Chen sold [18] baskets of oranges altogether.

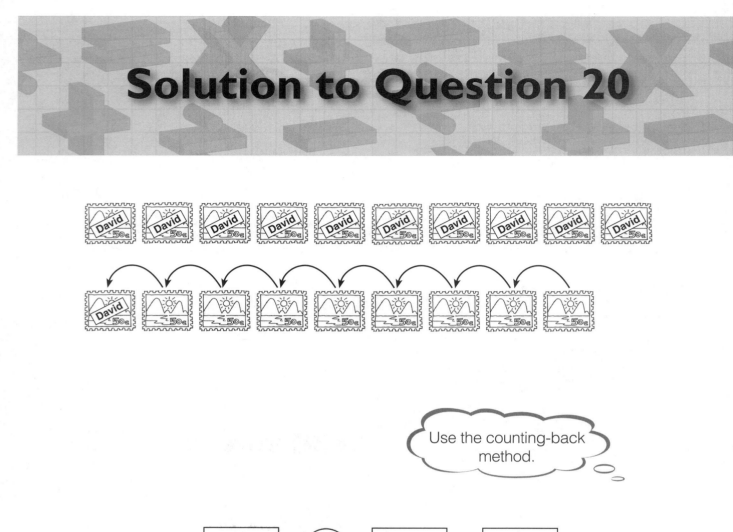

Use the counting-back method.

David has [11] stamps.

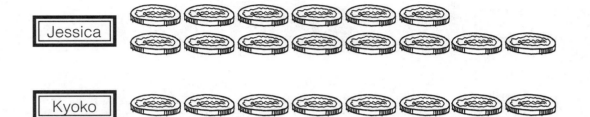

14 – 8

(4) (10)

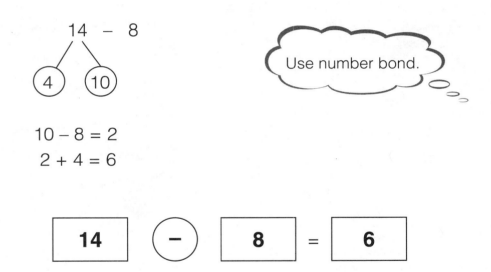

Use number bond.

10 – 8 = 2
2 + 4 = 6

| 14 | − | 8 | = | 6 |

Kyoko has (6) fewer coins than Jessica.

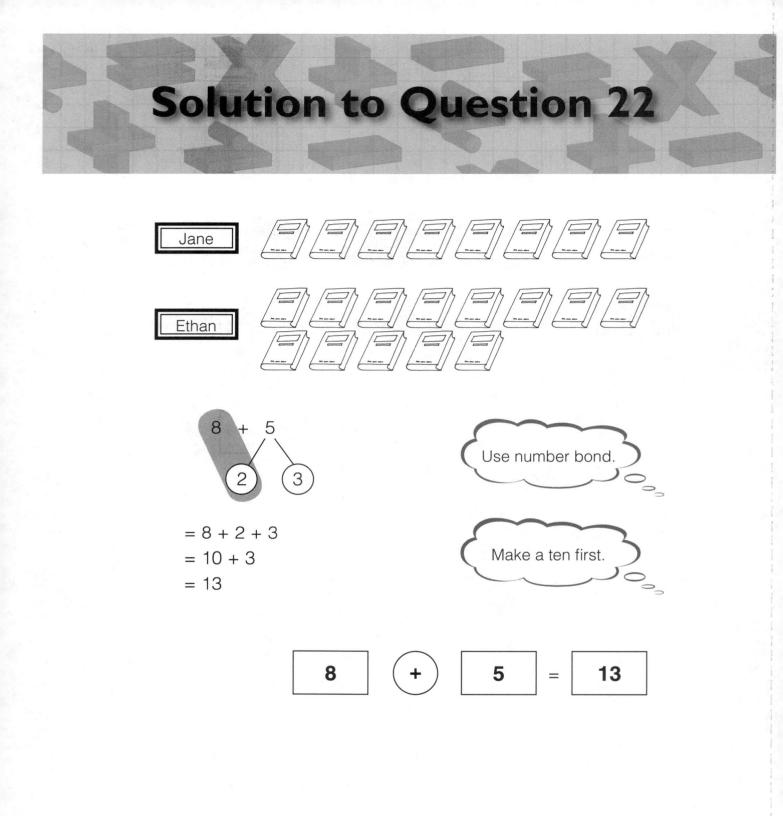

Jane

Ethan

8 + 5

2   3

= 8 + 2 + 3
= 10 + 3
= 13

Use number bond.

Make a ten first.

| 8 | + | 5 | = | 13 |

Ethan has **13** books.

Solution to Question 23

(a)

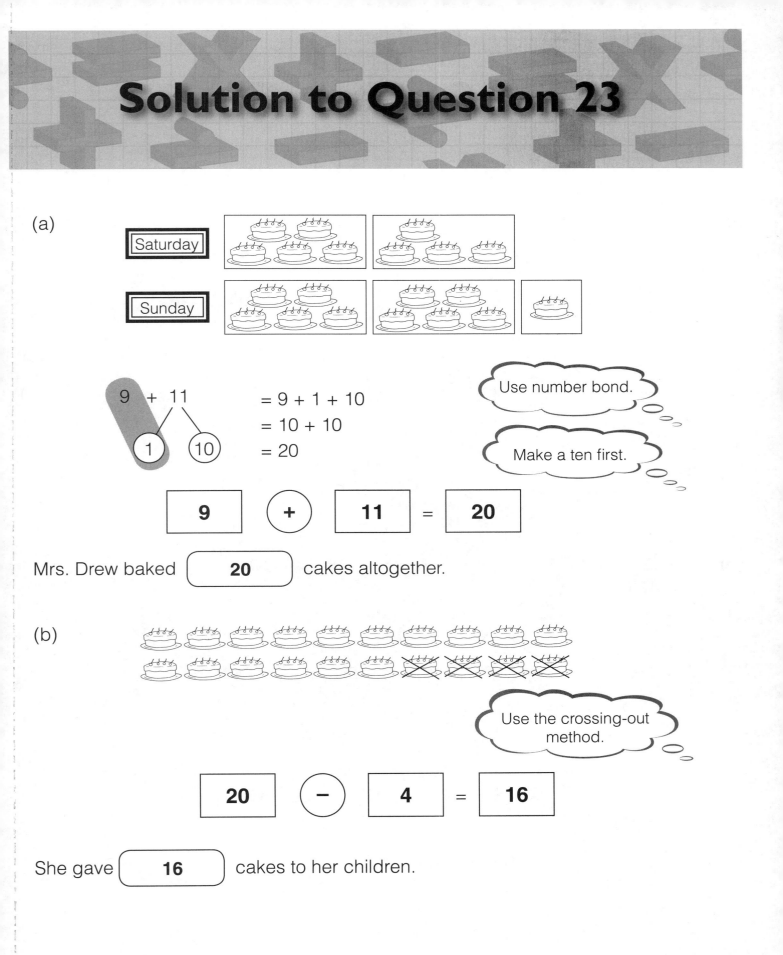

Saturday

Sunday

9 + 11
  1   10

= 9 + 1 + 10
= 10 + 10
= 20

Use number bond.

Make a ten first.

| **9** | **+** | **11** | = | **20** |

Mrs. Drew baked ⟨ **20** ⟩ cakes altogether.

(b)

Use the crossing-out method.

| **20** | **−** | **4** | = | **16** |

She gave ⟨ **16** ⟩ cakes to her children.

(a)

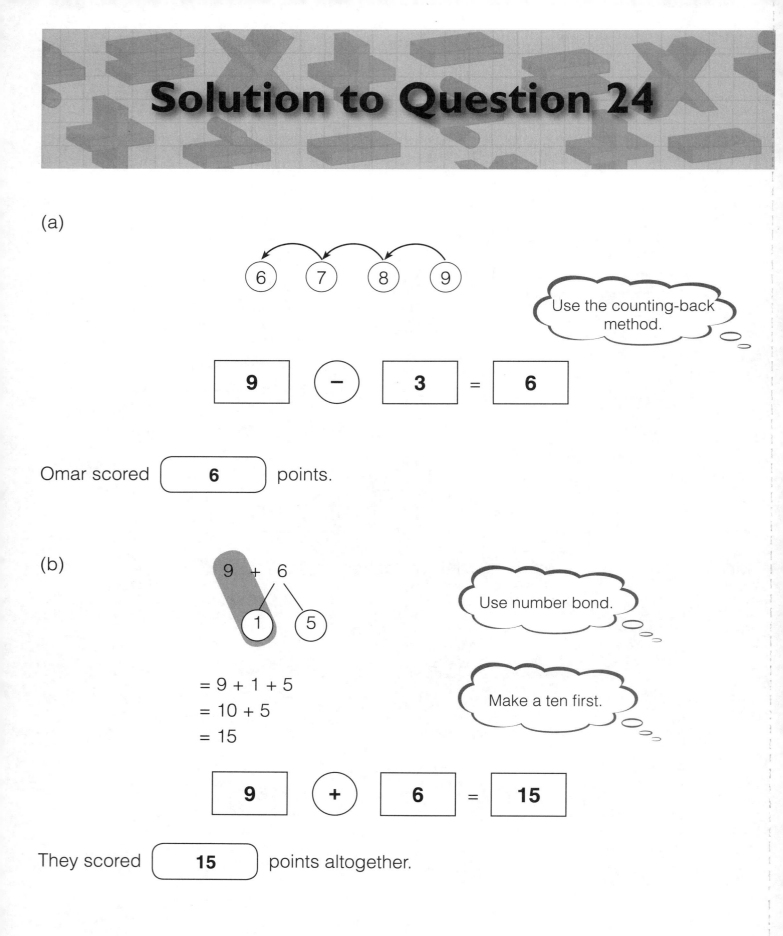

6 7 8 9

Use the counting-back method.

| 9 | − | 3 | = | 6 |

Omar scored 6 points.

(b)

9 + 6

1 5

Use number bond.

= 9 + 1 + 5
= 10 + 5
= 15

Make a ten first.

| 9 | + | 6 | = | 15 |

They scored 15 points altogether.

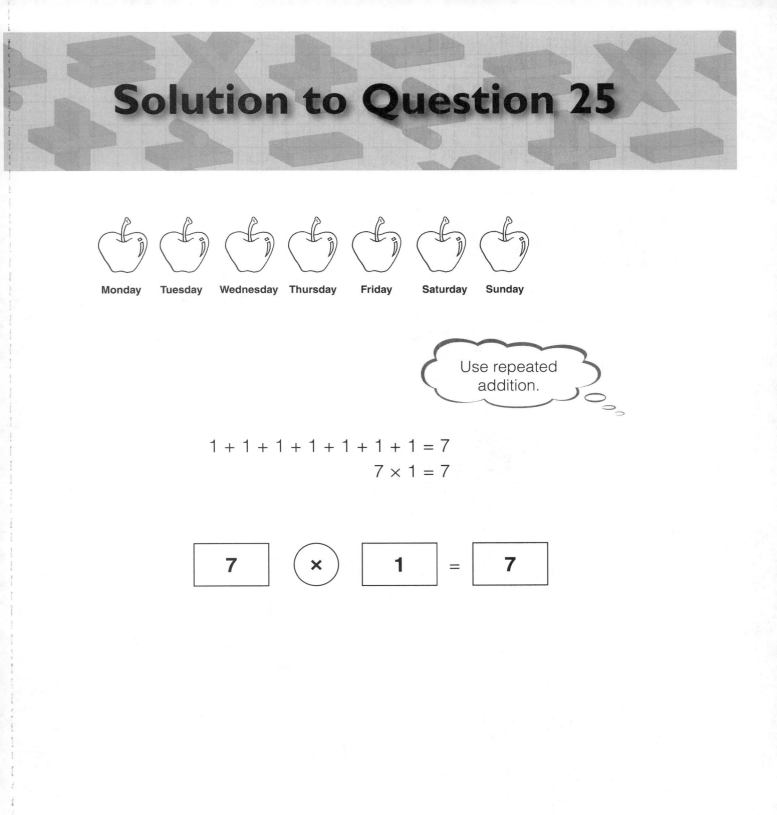

Monday Tuesday Wednesday Thursday Friday Saturday Sunday

Use repeated addition.

$$1 + 1 + 1 + 1 + 1 + 1 + 1 = 7$$
$$7 \times 1 = 7$$

7 × 1 = 7

Alex eats 7 apples in a week.

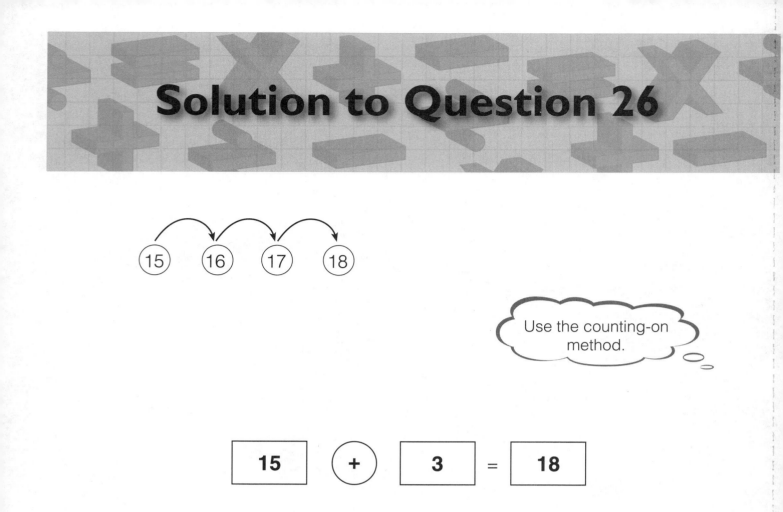

Jackson is (**18**) years old.

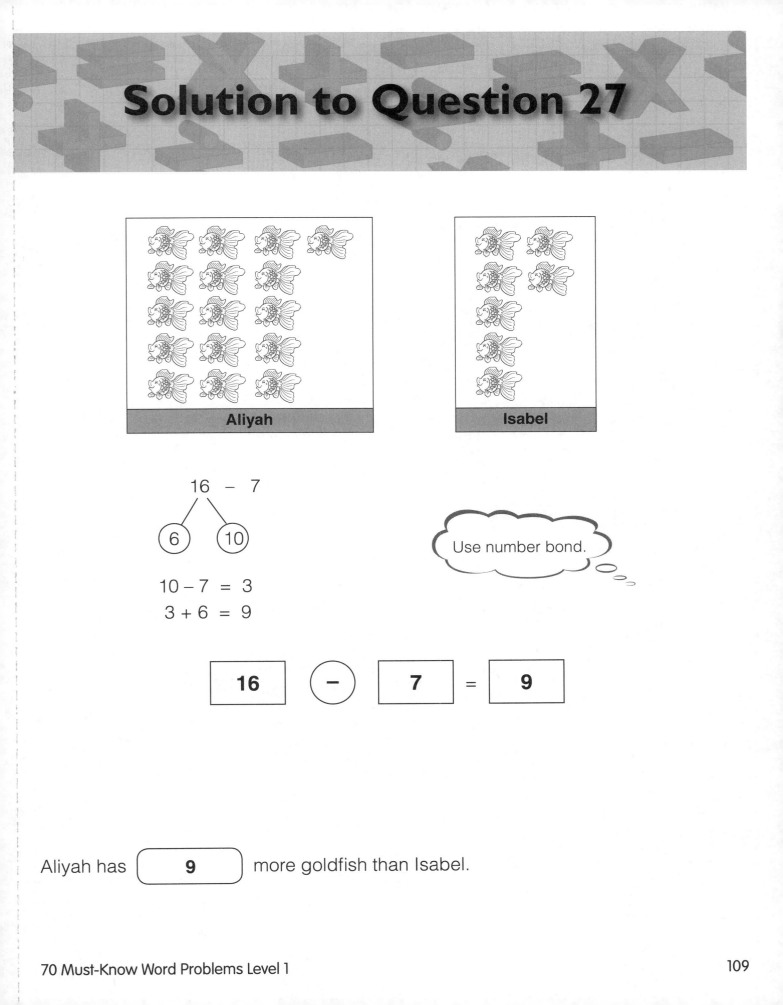

Aliyah

Isabel

16 – 7

6   10

10 – 7 = 3

3 + 6 = 9

Use number bond.

| **16** | – | **7** | = | **9** |

Aliyah has ⬭ **9** ⬭ more goldfish than Isabel.

Solution to Question 28

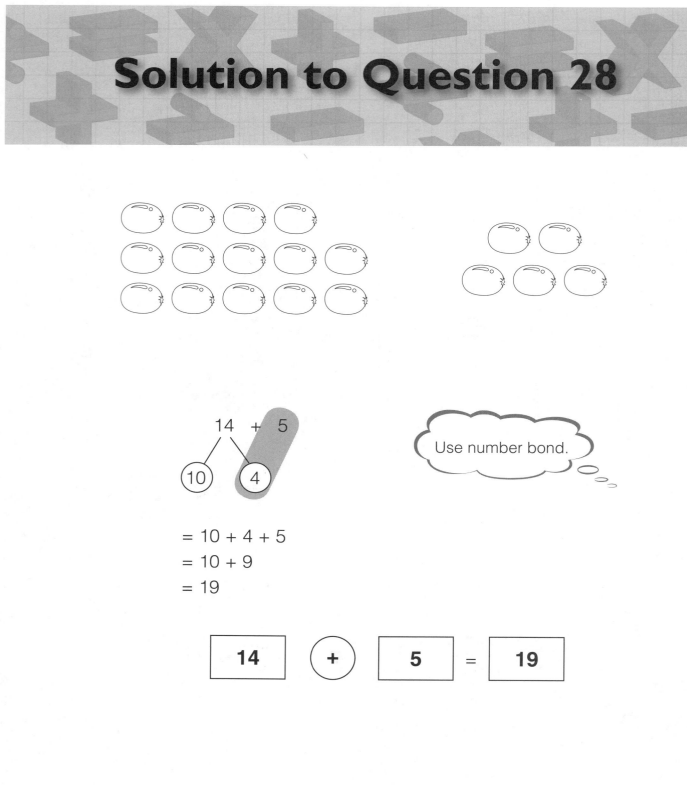

$$= 10 + 4 + 5$$
$$= 10 + 9$$
$$= 19$$

Use number bond.

$$\boxed{14} \;\; \bigoplus \;\; \boxed{5} \; = \; \boxed{19}$$

There are $\boxed{19}$ kiwis in the basket now.

Solution to Question 29

18 – 6

(8)   (10)

Use number bond.

10 – 6 = 4
4 + 8 = 12

| 18 | – | 6 | = | 12 |

There are [**12**] boys.

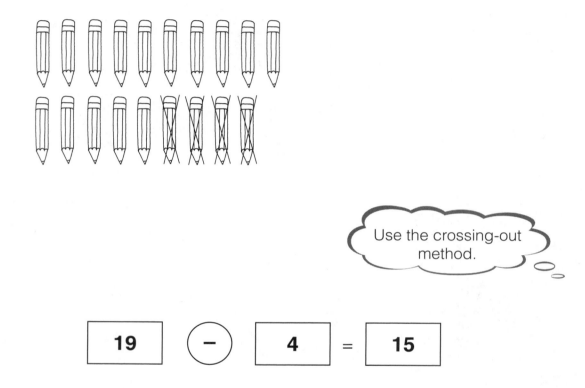

Use the crossing-out method.

$$19 \; - \; 4 = 15$$

Diego has 15 pencils left.

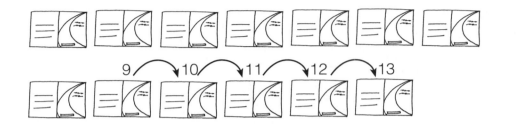

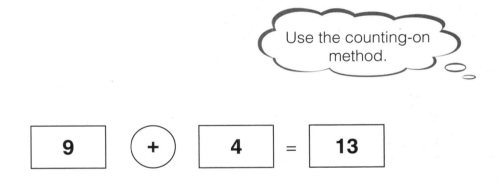

Use the counting-on method.

$$9 \enspace + \enspace 4 \enspace = \enspace 13$$

Benny has 13 cards.

13 – 4

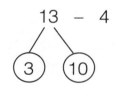

Use number bond.

10 – 4 = 6
6 + 3 = 9

| 13 | – | 4 | = | 9 |

There are 9 more chickens than ducks.

Solution to Question 33

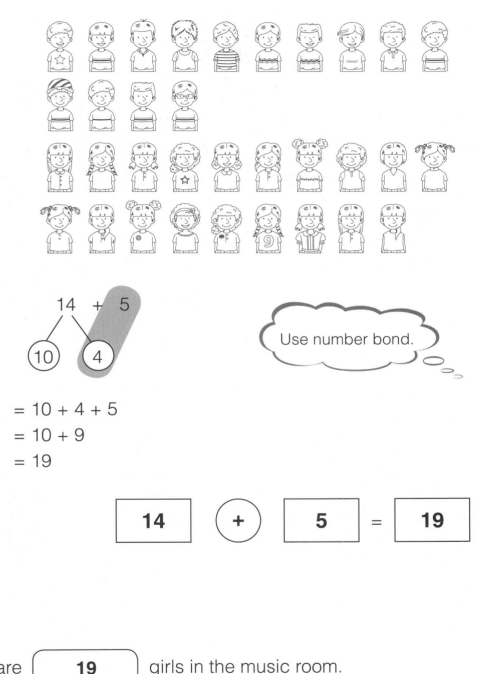

14 + 5

10   4

= 10 + 4 + 5
= 10 + 9
= 19

Use number bond.

14 (+) 5 = 19

There are [19] girls in the music room.

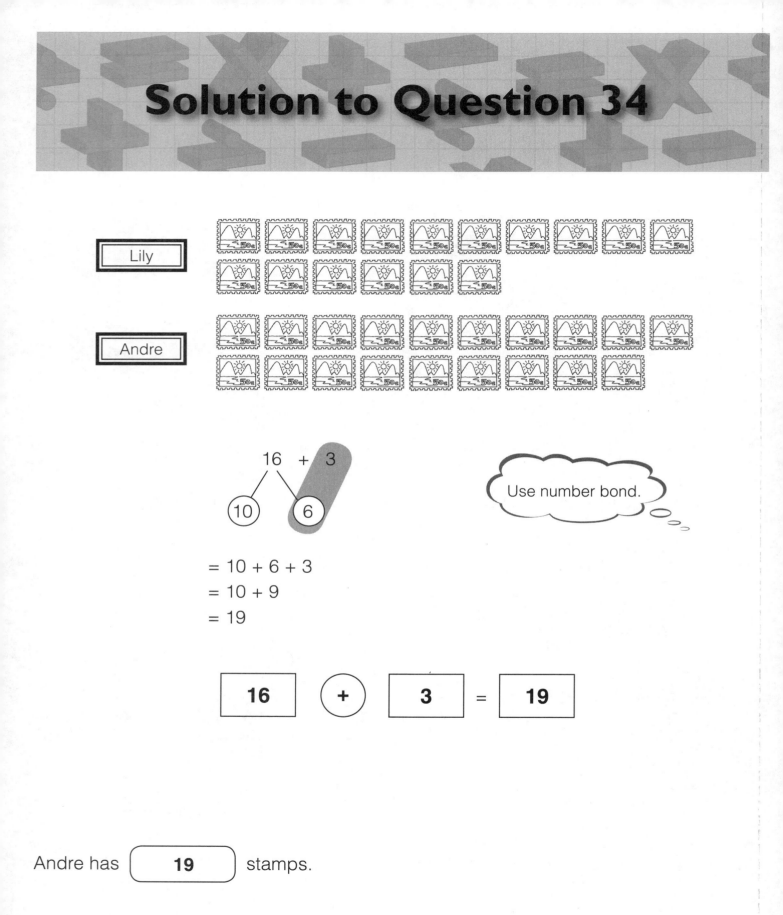

Lily

Andre

$$16 + 3$$
$$10 \quad 6$$

Use number bond.

= 10 + 6 + 3
= 10 + 9
= 19

| 16 | + | 3 | = | 19 |

Andre has ⌐ 19 ⌐ stamps.

Solution to Question 35

$$19 - 7$$

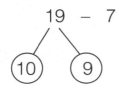

Use number bond.

$$9 - 7 = 2$$
$$2 + 10 = 12$$

$$\boxed{19} \; \bigcirc\!\!\!- \; \boxed{7} = \boxed{12}$$

There are $\boxed{12}$ men on the train.

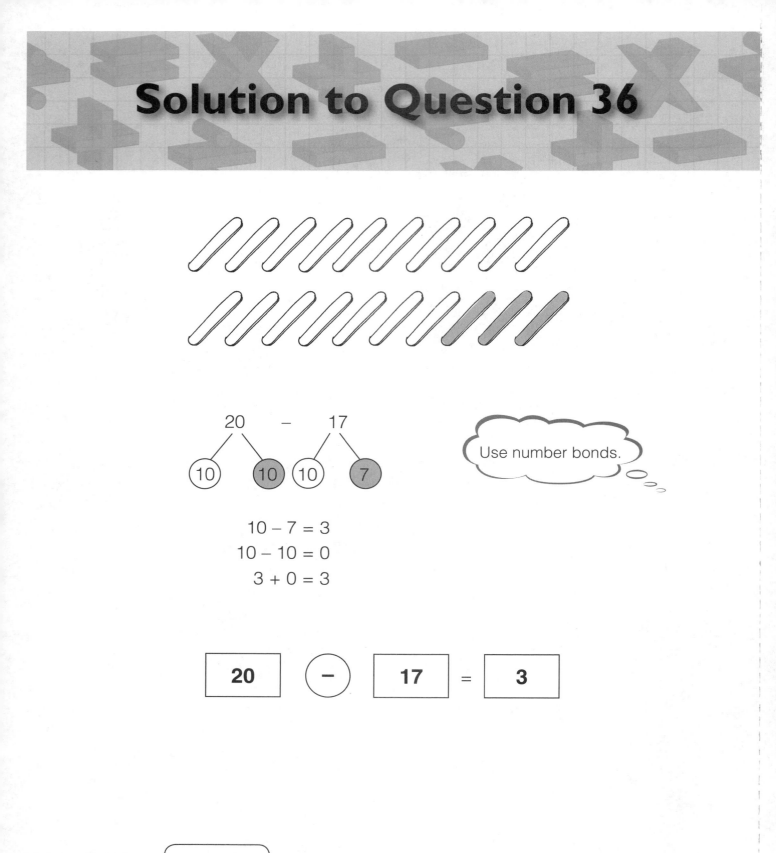

20 — 17

(10) (10) (10) (7)

Use number bonds.

10 − 7 = 3
10 − 10 = 0
3 + 0 = 3

| 20 | − | 17 | = | 3 |

He must collect 3 more ice-cream sticks.

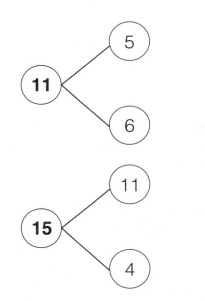

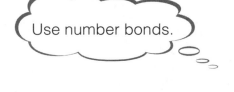

Use number bonds.

$$5 \; (+) \; 6 \; (+) \; 4 \; = \; 15$$

Sophia has (**15**) bows altogether.

20 – 8

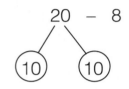

Use number bond.

10 – 8 = 2
2 + 10 = 12

| 20 | – | 8 | = | 12 |

Akiko's babysitter is [**12**] years older than Akiko.

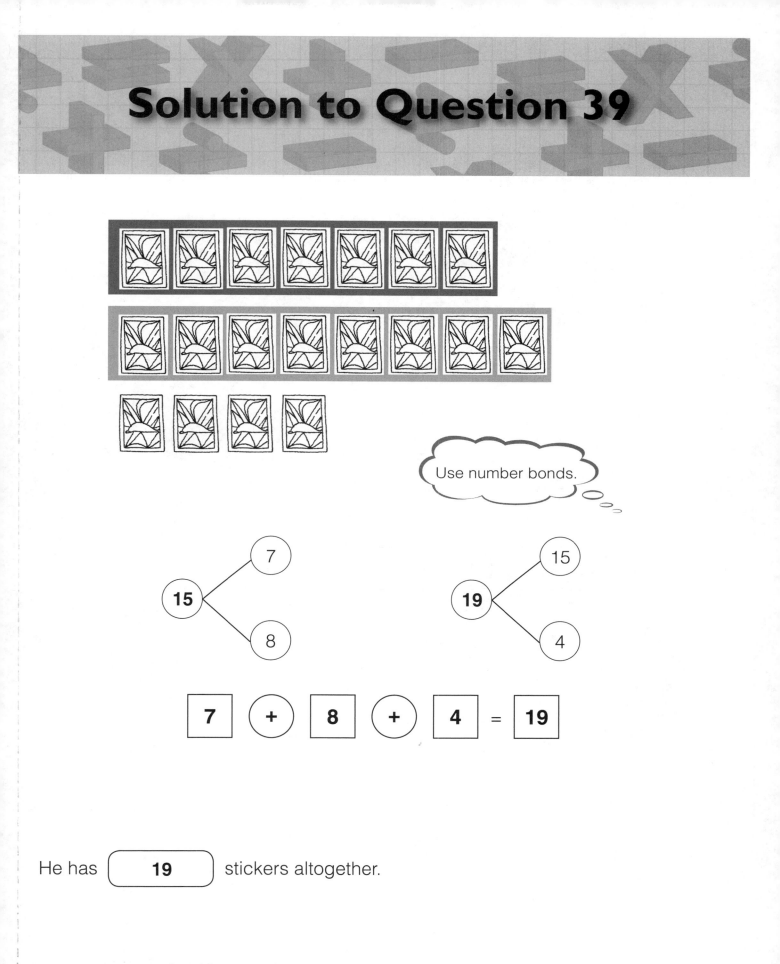

Use number bonds.

7 + 8 + 4 = 19

He has [**19**] stickers altogether.

Solution to Question 40

Use repeated addition.

$$4 + 4 + 4 + 4 = 16$$
$$4 \times 4 = 16$$

$$\boxed{4} \enspace \bigcirc\!\!\!\!\!\times \enspace \boxed{4} \enspace = \enspace \boxed{16}$$

4 cats have [**16**] legs.

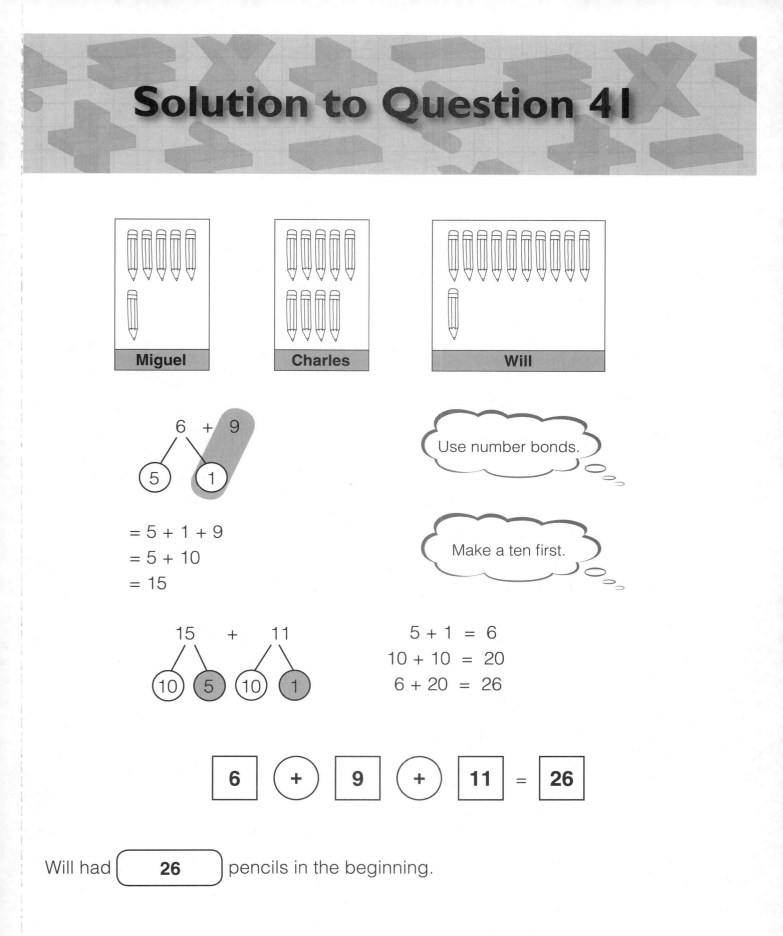

| Miguel | Charles | Will |

$6 + 9$

(5) (1)

$= 5 + 1 + 9$
$= 5 + 10$
$= 15$

Use number bonds.

Make a ten first.

15   +   11

(10) (5) (10) (1)

$5 + 1 = 6$
$10 + 10 = 20$
$6 + 20 = 26$

| 6 | + | 9 | + | 11 | = | 26 |

Will had **26** pencils in the beginning.

20 – 7

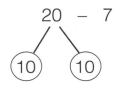

10 – 7 = 3

3 + 10 = 13

Use number bond.

| **20** | – | **7** | = | **13** |

13 boys do not wear glasses.

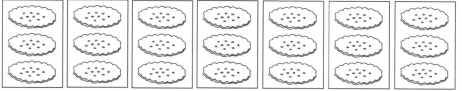

Use repeated addition.

$$3 + 3 + 3 + 3 + 3 + 3 + 3 = 21$$
$$7 \times 3 = 21$$

| 7 | × | 3 | = | 21 |

She bought [21] crackers in all.

Solution to Question 44

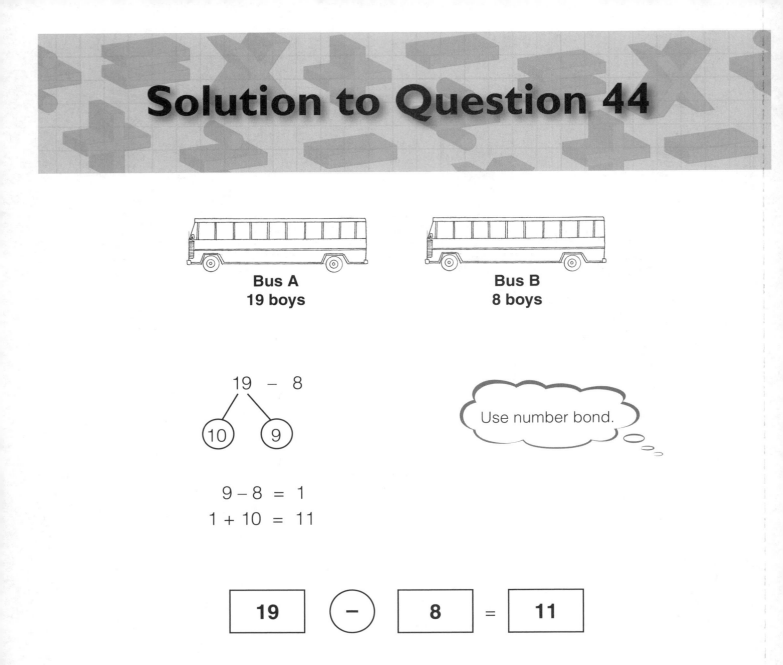

Bus A
19 boys

Bus B
8 boys

19 – 8

⑩   ⑨

Use number bond.

9 – 8 = 1
1 + 10 = 11

| 19 | (–) | 8 | = | 11 |

There are [**11**] more boys on Bus A than on Bus B.

Solution to Question 45

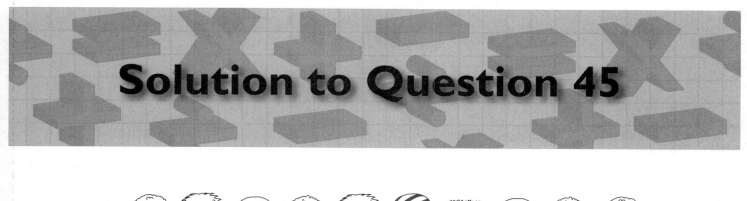

Absent

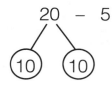

20 – 5

(10) (10)

Use number bond.

10 – 5 = 5
5 + 10 = 15

| 20 | – | 5 | = | 15 |

15 students came to class.

Solution to Question 46

$5 + 5 + 5 + 5 = 20$

$4 \times 5 = 20$

Use repeated addition.

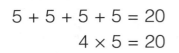 

| 4 | × | 5 | = | 20 |

She has [**20**] oranges in all.

15 – 9

⑤ ⑩

Use number bond.

10 – 9 = 1
1 + 5 = 6

| 15 | ⊝ | 9 | = | 6 |

She needs ⟨ 6 ⟩ more sacks of flour.

$$16 - 8$$

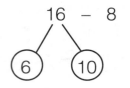

6   10

Use number bond.

$$10 - 8 = 2$$
$$2 + 6 = 8$$

| 16 | $-$ | 8 | = | 8 |

Kenny has (8) erasers.

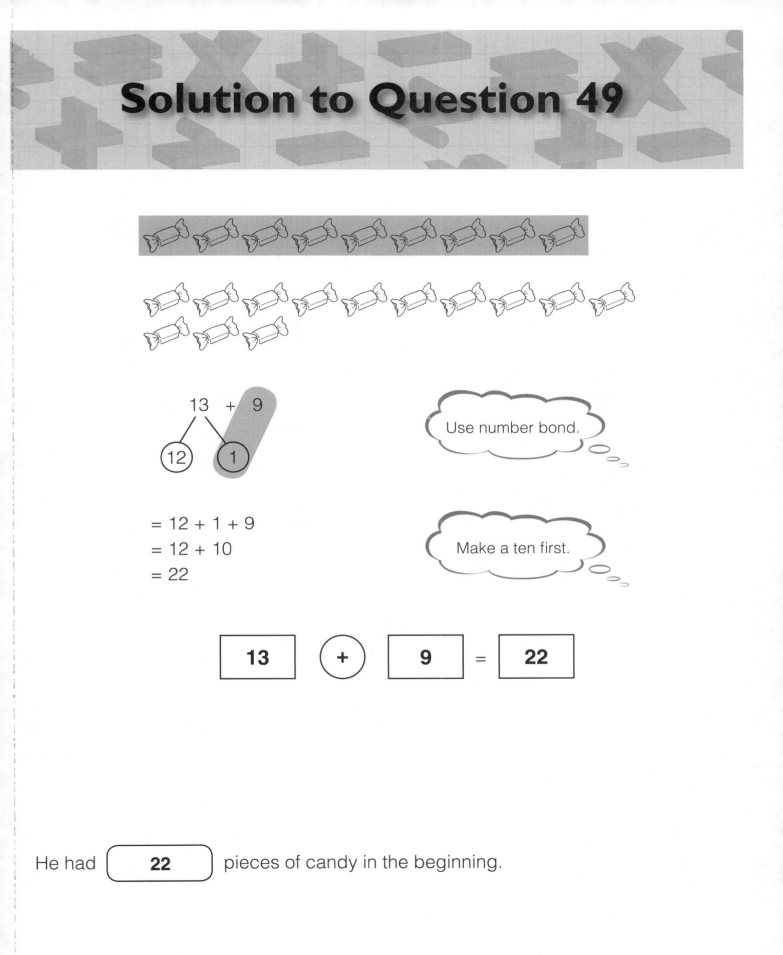

13 + 9

12   1

Use number bond.

= 12 + 1 + 9
= 12 + 10
= 22

Make a ten first.

$$\boxed{13} \; \bigoplus \; \boxed{9} \; = \; \boxed{22}$$

He had (**22**) pieces of candy in the beginning.

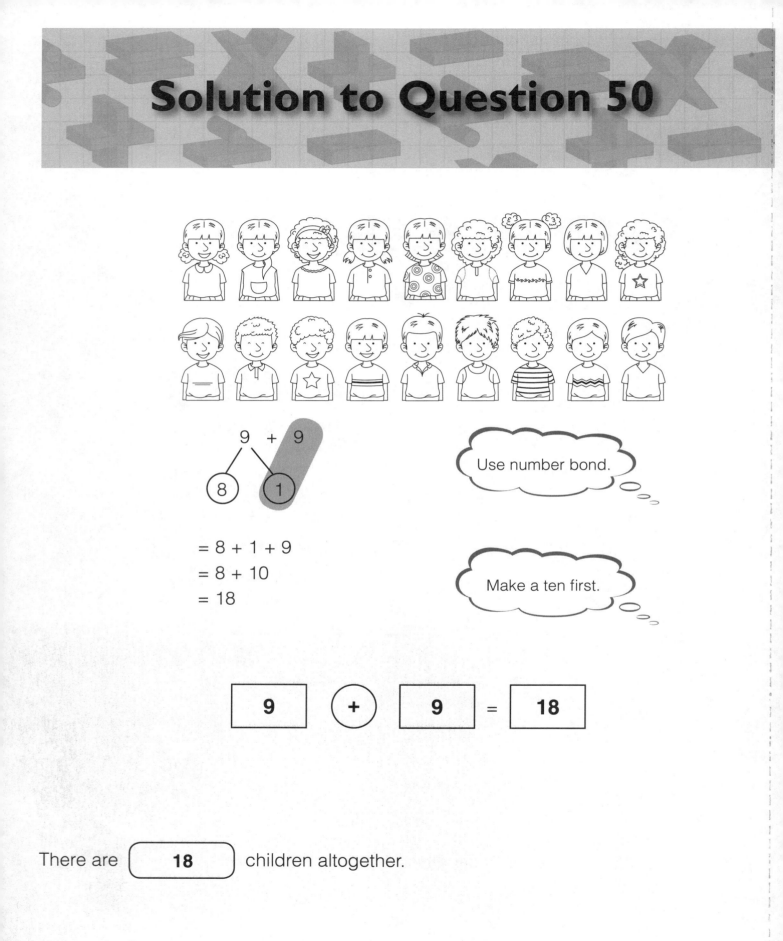

9 + 9

8   1

Use number bond.

= 8 + 1 + 9
= 8 + 10
= 18

Make a ten first.

| 9 | (+) | 9 | = | 18 |

There are [18] children altogether.

Solution to Question 51

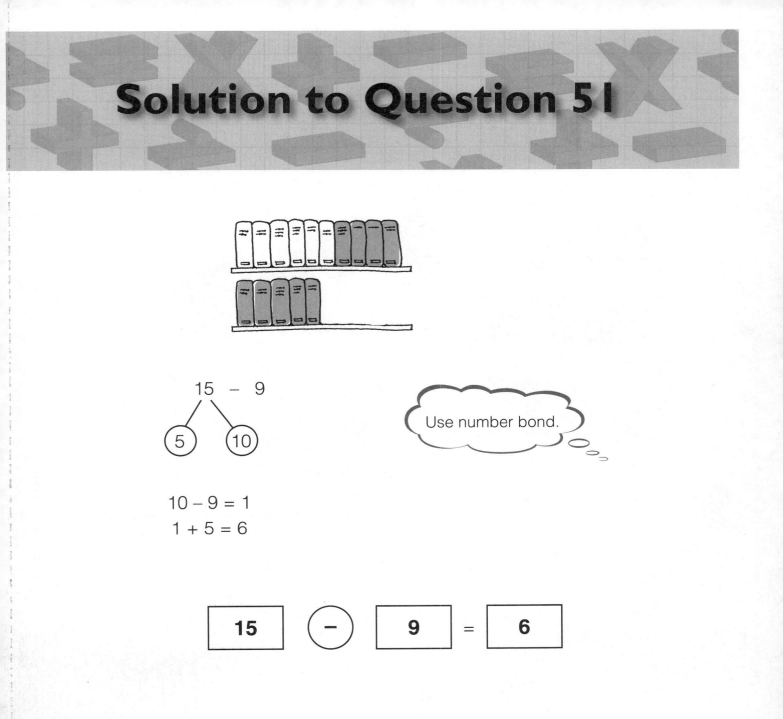

15 − 9

5   10

Use number bond.

10 − 9 = 1
1 + 5 = 6

15 ⊖ 9 = 6

There are   6   English books.

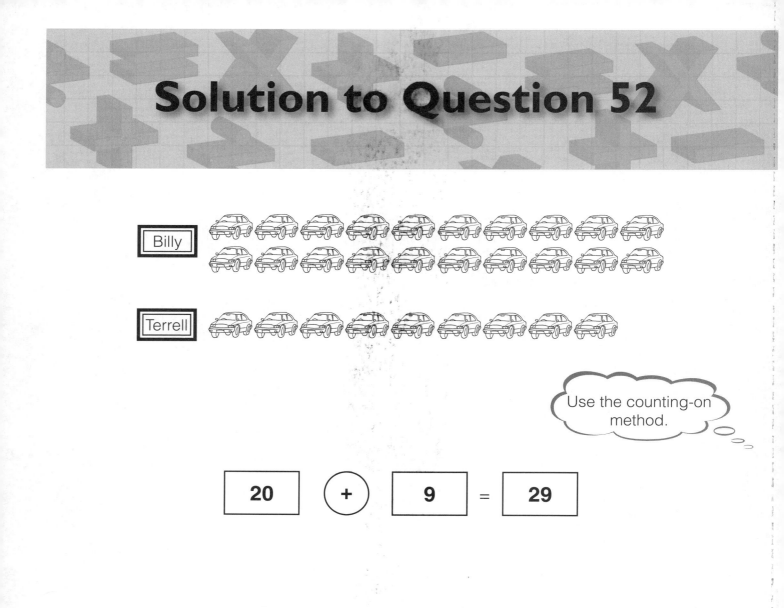

$$\boxed{20} \;\; \bigoplus \;\; \boxed{9} \;\; = \;\; \boxed{29}$$

They have 〔 **29** 〕 toy cars altogether.

Solution to Question 53

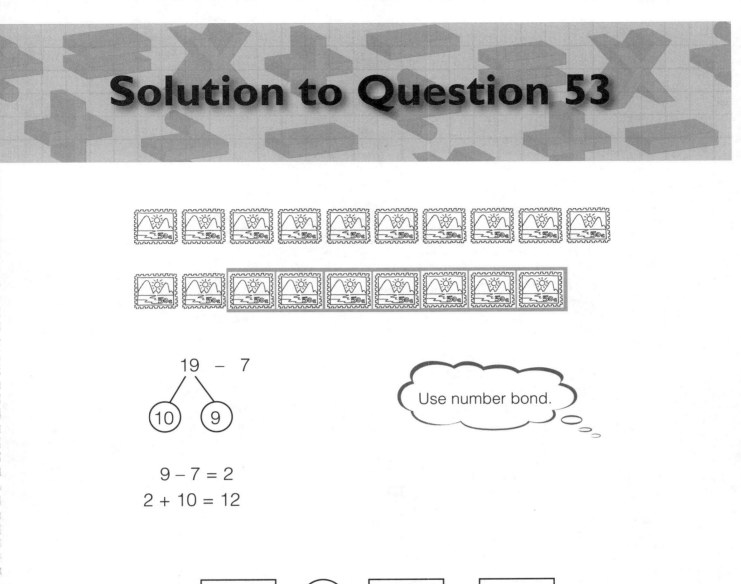

19 – 7

(10) (9)

9 – 7 = 2
2 + 10 = 12

Use number bond.

| **19** | – | **7** | = | **12** |

She shares [**12**] stamps with her brother and sister.

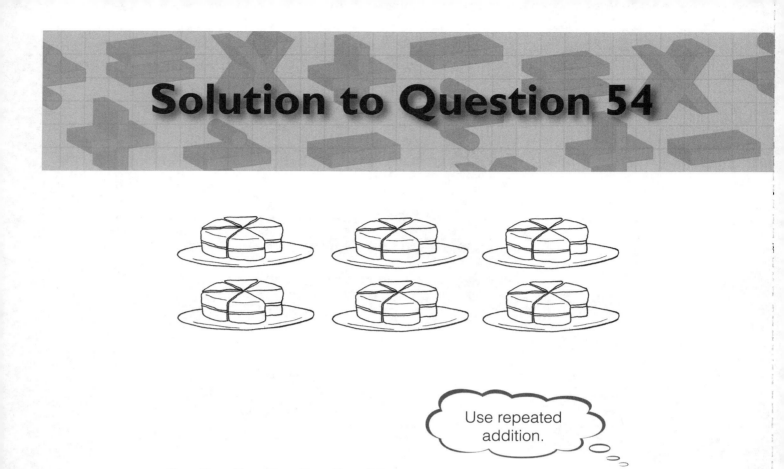

Use repeated addition.

$$5 + 5 + 5 + 5 + 5 + 5 = 30$$
$$6 \times 5 = 30$$

$$\boxed{6} \enspace \bigotimes \enspace \boxed{5} = \boxed{30}$$

There are $\boxed{30}$ pieces of cake altogether.

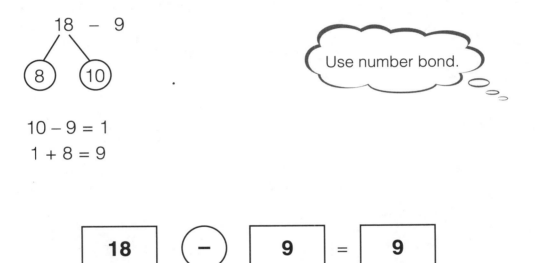

$$18 - 9$$

8   10

10 − 9 = 1
1 + 8 = 9

Use number bond.

18   −   9   =   9

He had [9] watermelons left.

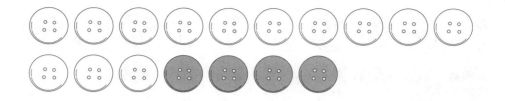

17 – 4

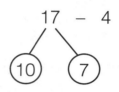

Use number bond.

7 – 4 = 3

3 + 10 = 13

Mei had 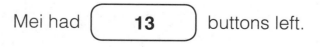 buttons left.

13

(a)

40 – 16

(30) (10) (10) (6)

Use number bonds.

10 – 6 = 4
30 – 10 = 20
4 + 20 = 24

| 40 | (–) | 16 | = | 24 |

Colin has [24] stickers.

(b)

24 – 9

(14) (10)

Use number bond.

10 – 9 = 1
1 + 14 = 15

| 24 | (–) | 9 | = | 15 |

Colin has [15] stickers now.

Solution to Question 58

$$5 + 5 + 5 = 15$$
$$3 \times 5 = 15$$

Use repeated addition.

| 3 | × | 5 | = | 15 |

There are (15) children in 3 groups.

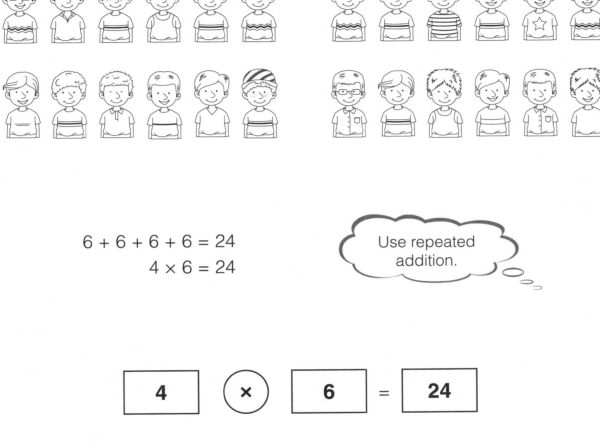

$$6 + 6 + 6 + 6 = 24$$
$$4 \times 6 = 24$$

Use repeated addition.

| **4** | × | **6** | = | **24** |

There are **24** boys altogether.

8 + 8 + 8 + 8 = 32

4 × 8 = 32

Use repeated addition.

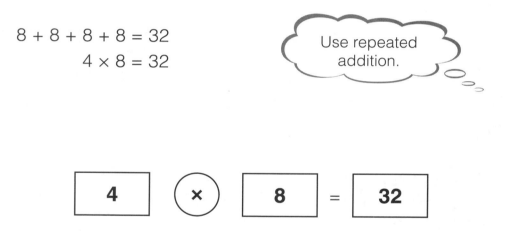

| 4 | × | 8 | = | 32 |

His mother is (**32**) years old.

10 – 5 = 5
30 – 10 = 20
5 + 20 = 25

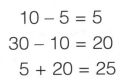

| 40 | $-$ | 15 | = | 25 |

She had (**25**) coins in the beginning.

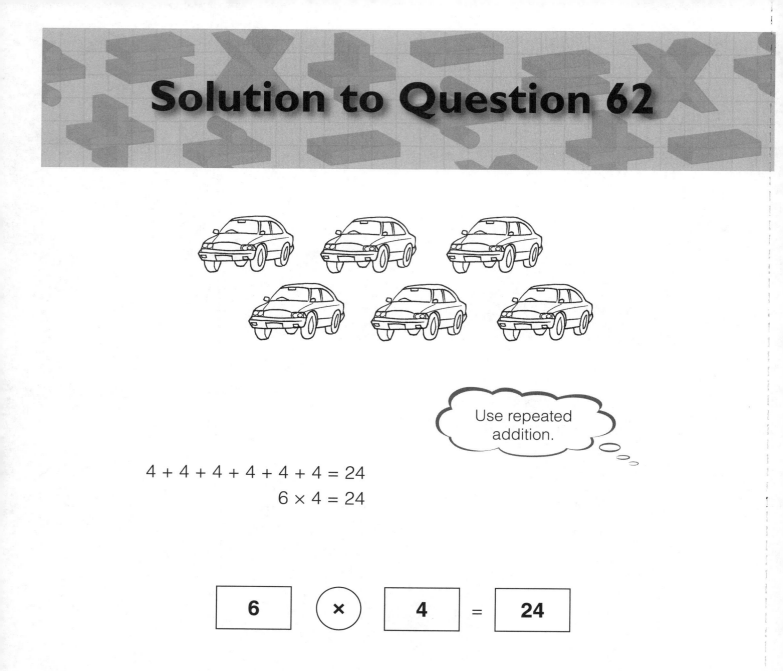

Use repeated addition.

$4 + 4 + 4 + 4 + 4 + 4 = 24$

$6 \times 4 = 24$

$$\boxed{6} \;\; \bigcirc\!\!\!\times \;\; \boxed{4} \;\; = \;\; \boxed{24}$$

There are ⟨ **24** ⟩ wheels altogether.

Solution to Question 63

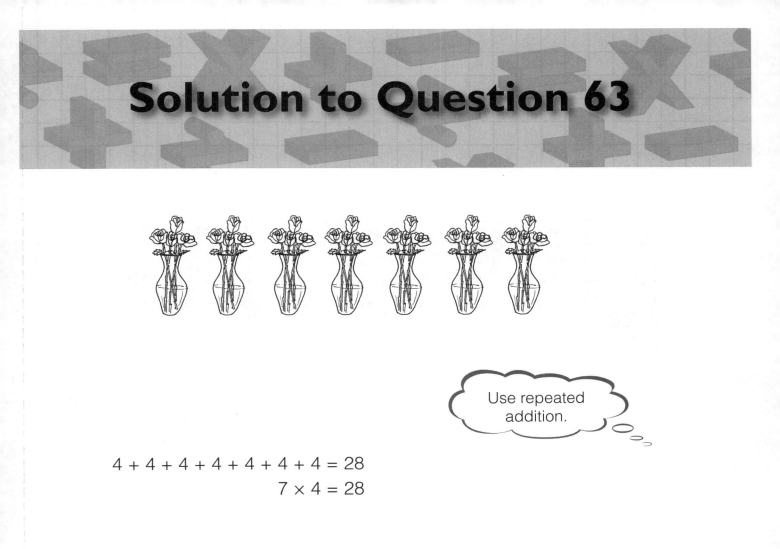

Use repeated addition.

4 + 4 + 4 + 4 + 4 + 4 + 4 = 28

7 × 4 = 28

$$7 \quad \times \quad 4 \quad = \quad 28$$

There are  **28** roses altogether.

Solution to Question 64

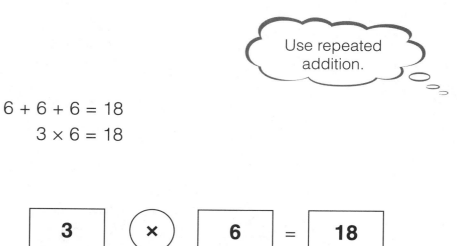

Use repeated addition.

$6 + 6 + 6 = 18$

$3 \times 6 = 18$

$$\boxed{3} \; \otimes \; \boxed{6} = \boxed{18}$$

They bought (**18**) movie tickets in all.

Solution to Question 65

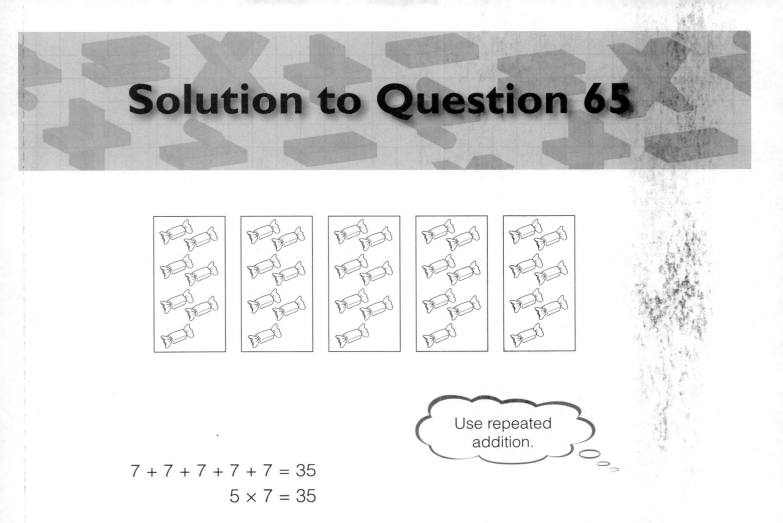

Use repeated addition.

$7 + 7 + 7 + 7 + 7 = 35$

$5 \times 7 = 35$

There are [**35**] pieces of candy altogether.

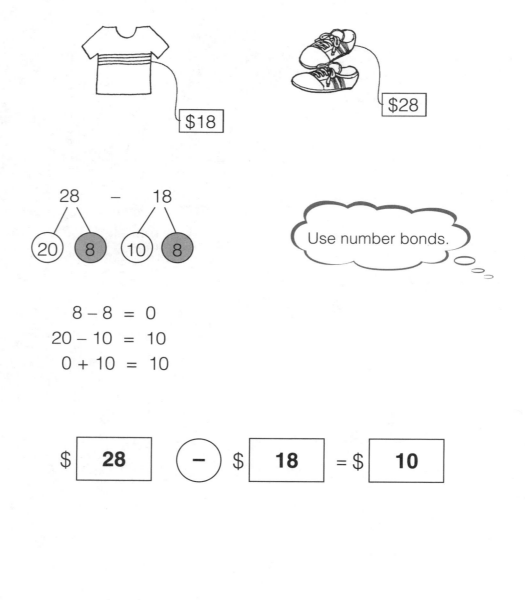

The pair of shoes costs $ 10 more than the T-shirt.

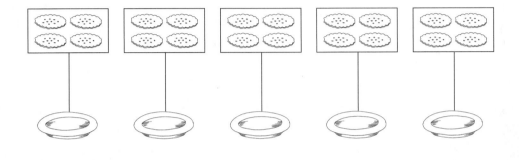

Use the grouping method.

She needs (**5**) plates.

50 cents   90 cents

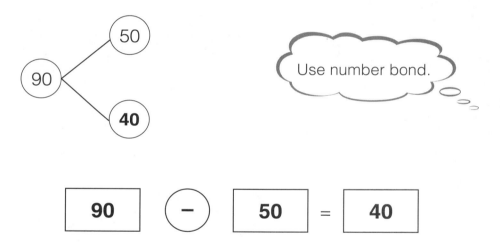

Use number bond.

| 90 | − | 50 | = | 40 |

The pencil is (**40**) cents cheaper.

Use the grouping method.

Each child got (**4**) strawberries.

Solution to Question 70

Alyssa

Ling

Connor

Julio

Use the grouping method.

Each child got (**3**) beads.

Notes

Notes

Notes

Notes

Notes

Notes

Notes

Notes